EMERGENCY POWERS, COVID-19 RESTRICTIONS AND MANDATORY VACCINATION

A 'RULE-OF-LAW' PERSPECTIVE

Augusto Zimmermann

Gabriël Moens AM

Connor Court Publishing

Published by Connor Court Publishing Pty Ltd

PO Box 7257
Redland Bay QLD 4165
sales@connorcourt.com
www.connorcourt.com

ISBN: 9781922449948

Cover design by Maria Giordano

Front Cover painting: 'The Chinchillas', 1799. Artist: Francisco Goya.

Posted in 'Los Caprichos'. Los Caprichos were published in 1799 at a time of social/political repression and economic crisis in Spain. The series is evidence of the artist's political liberalism and revulsion towards ignorance and intellectual oppression.

Dedicated to all politicians and scholars who, in an illiberal era of Australia's history, courageously distinguish between the 'rule of law' and 'arbitrary rule by executive decree'.

CONTENTS

1

THE EMERGING CONTROVERSY

Since March 2020, Australia's governments have been using their powers to excessively coerce, obstruct or otherwise unreasonably interfere with the life, liberty, movement, and property of the citizen. These governments are exercising *emergency powers* to impose measures that profoundly undermine basic principles of the rule of law. At present, government authorities are trying to achieve the goal of full vaccination by coercing, scaring, threatening, and punishing the Australian people.

The health orders issued by Australia's governments have the effect of violating the concept of legality, known as the 'rule of law'. These governments have adopted extra-constitutional measures that undermine the doctrine of separation of powers and the principle of equality before the law, as well as the basic right of citizens to object to any form of medical treatment, including mandatory vaccinations, which are now increasingly imposed by the government. These mandates are enforced either directly, by coercive measures, or indirectly, by distributing burdens and benefits on the ground of the person's vaccine status.

Australia's COVID-19 journey started at the end of January 2020 when the first death was recorded in Perth, Western

Australia, of a 78-year-old passenger who contracted the disease on the cruise ship, The Princess Diamond. A National Cabinet was formed on 13 March 2020 to respond to the Covid challenge. This Cabinet consists of the Prime Minister, who chairs the meetings of the Cabinet, the Premiers of the States and Chief Ministers of the Territories, assisted by the Chief Medical Health Officer. Although the Cabinet initially concentrated on the management of the COVID-19 health crisis, it has now shifted its focus to Australia's economic recovery and jobs creation programs.

Initially, Australian States relied on lockdowns and border closures to slow, or to eliminate, the spread of the COVID-19 virus and its variants. These measures were promised to be only temporary, and they were welcomed by the electorate that returned the governments of Queensland and Tasmania to power, and the government of Western Australia, led by Premier Mark McGowan, obliterated the Liberal Opposition in the last State election held in March 2021.

However, support for lockdowns and border closures is not without its critics. For example, Martin Kulldorff, professor of medicine at Harvard University, Sunetra Gupta, professor of theoretical epidemiology at Oxford University, and Jay Bhattacharya, professor of medicine at Stanford University, have highlighted "the damaging physical and mental health impacts of the prevailing COVID-19 policies."[1] These professors, all noted epidemiologists, have issued the *Great Barrington Declaration*, arguing that "lockdown policies are producing devastating effects on short and long-term public health."

These professors are experts in epidemiology and teach in three of the world's most prestigious universities. They argue that, while it would be easy to expose the economic ravages caused by lockdowns and border closures, any criticisms of these measures should rationally focus on their effect on the health of the population. Their research points to "lower childhood vaccination rates, worsening cardiovascular disease outcomes, fewer cancer screenings and deteriorating mental health – leading to greater excess mortality in years to come, with the working class and younger members of society carrying the heaviest burden." The Declaration then recommends the adoption of an approach called 'Focused Protection', which involves allowing "those who are at minimal risk of death to live their lives normally to build up immunity to the virus through natural infection, while better protecting those who are at highest risk."

The importance of the epidemiologists' recommendation lies in its ability to secure a long-term solution to the alleged pandemic, whereas lockdowns and border closures are merely reactive short-term temporary measures that seek to limit the spread of the virus. They are, however, measures that happened with monotonous regularity in Australia. The lockdowns and border closures have prevented a rational discussion on the impact of the disease on various classes of people, especially young Australians, while disregarding the special needs of vulnerable citizens, older people, disabled people, and people in care facilities. Of course, any responses to the COVID-19 challenge are fraught with serious problems. The inability or unwillingness to rationally consider all appropriate responses and strategies to fight the spread of the disease may well be one of the casualties of the government's strategy.

However, when vaccines, including AstraZeneca, Pfizer, and Moderna became available, Australian governments, embarked on an ambitious program of vaccinating the Australian people. It promised to relax the restrictions and to abandon lockdowns and border closures, provided at least 80 per cent of the population was vaccinated with a first and second dose. Most States and Territories were on track to achieve, and to exceed, the goal of an 80 percent vaccination rate before the end of 2021. The Australian government is now also encouraging those who are vaccinated to get a booster shot, available five months after the second vaccination.

To reach or to surpass the goal of 80 per cent of fully vaccinated people, States have started to embrace vaccine mandates as the way out of lockdowns and border closures and to facilitate a return to life as it was prior to the emergence of the COVID-19 virus. These States have already decided that the unvaccinated will be treated differently to the vaccinated. In practice, this means that unvaccinated citizens will have less freedoms to travel and to socialise, or even to go to restaurants and attend football matches, or music festivals. These indications have fuelled the media's doomsday predictions that point to the development of a two-tier Australian society, where the equal treatment of all Australians is but a reminder of the past.

In this context, unvaccinated people have already been barred from locations, dismissed from their jobs under a 'no jab, no job' policy, and denied movement freedoms. In the same vein, businesses that accept unvaccinated people can be subject to exceptionally heavy fines. Private employers have been encouraged to require their workforce to be fully vaccinated. For example, Qantas has announced that all people who want to fly internationally, including its workforce, will need to possess a certificate of vaccination. Similarly, the University of Queensland intends to enforce a vaccination order for all staff, students, and visitors, who will be attending its campus at the start of the first semester in February 2022. Also in Queensland, as from 17 December 2021, unvaccinated people are no longer allowed to visit clubs, restaurants, cafés, theatres, museums, and libraries. Even supermarkets will have the option to exclude unvaccinated customers. These orders have turned Australia into a deeply illiberal society, where some people are more equal than others. Such draconian and totalitarian measures have never been implemented before in Australia. Any legitimate responses to the creation of an illiberal Australia are discussed in Chapter Seven of this book.

Recently, Dr Mattias Desmet of the Ghent University in Belgium has argued that "historical analysis shows that so-called 'mass formation' can be the first step toward totalitarianism and atrocity in the name of collective welfare." Ashley Sadler, commenting upon Desmet's views notes that, "Discriminatory lockdowns, 'show me your papers' policies, mandatory quarantines for healthy people, and incomprehensible police brutality against anti-lockdown protesters who merely want their lives back have demonstrated that those who worried more about the creeping rise of a totalitarian health dictatorship were far more correct than those who panicked about what was supposed to be the worst pandemic since the Spanish flu."[2] She rhetorically asks why "does our luxurious modern society appear to be marching toward the demonization and ostracization (or worse) of those opposed to the dominant regime?"

Dr Desmet argues that the response to the COVID-19 pandemic is an example of the psychological concept of "mass formation, a kind of broad scale hypnosis that causes large groups of people to band together to fight a common enemy with complete lack of concern for the loss of individual rights, privileges, and even well-being." It leads to "a kind of mental intoxication of connectedness, which is the real reason why people continue to buy into the narrative, even if it's utterly absurd or blatantly wrong." The 'mass formation', fuelled by COVID-19 restrictions and vaccine mandates, facilitates the creation of a two-tier Australia where some people will be more privileged than others, involving the distribution of burdens and benefits simply on the ground of peoples' vaccine status. This approach is unsupported by the *Nuremberg Code* – an ethics code – relied upon during the Nazi doctors' trials in Nuremberg in 1947. This Code has as its first principle the willingness and informed consent by the individual to receive medical treatment or to participate in a medical experiment.

One of the primary goals of the judicial function is to protect citizens against any adverse impact on their enjoyment of fundamental legal rights. This classic definition of judicial power, from which numerous court decisions have proceeded, is found in the 1909 case of *Huddart, Parker & Co Pty Ltd v Moorehead.*[3] There the nation's first Chief Justice, Samuel Griffith, explained that the words 'judicial power' as used in section 71 of the Constitution mean the power of the courts to protect fundamental rights related to life, liberty, or property. Chief Justice Griffith's definition referred to three basic elements of the judicial function: controversy; impact upon life, liberty, or property; and conclusiveness of the decision.

Although it is not feasible to predict what the nation's highest court, the High Court of Australia, might do if it were called upon to consider the constitutionality of vaccination orders and emergency measures, it is still possible to determine how the Constitution should be interpreted. Of course, the Australian Constitution must be interpreted in a manner that promotes its purposes, values, and principles. The Court, in assessing the constitutionality of these vaccine mandates, should consider that the primary purpose of a constitution, based on the principles of liberal democracy and representative government, is the establishment of a system of checks and balances capable of limiting arbitrary power and ensuring the realisation of the principle of legality, known as the 'rule of law'.

Mandatory vaccination, which is now steadily underway in

Australia to combat the spread of COVID-19, sits uncomfortably with the jurisprudence of the High Court and our traditions of constitutional government. One would expect the Court to acknowledge these basic traditions, and that discrimination on the grounds of vaccination amounts to a violation of the spirit of the Australian Constitution.

This monograph introduces its readers to the concept of legality known as the 'rule of law' (Chapter Two) and the use of emergency powers in Australia (Chapter Three). It focuses on an interpretation of section 51(xxiiiA) to assess the constitutionality of mandatory vaccination (Chapter Four). It then examines the use of the external affairs power found in section 51(xxix) of the Constitution to combat vaccination mandates (Chapter Five). The book considers paternalism as a principle of legislation in the imposition of vaccination mandates (Chapter Six). The role that civil disobedience can play when protesting the imposition of mandatory vaccination is discussed in this monograph (Chapter Seven). The reader is invited to ponder the great lessons learnt from the totalitarian past of Nazi Germany (Chapter Eight), before offering final considerations to conclude the monograph (Chapter Nine).

2

GOVERNMENT UNDER THE

'RULE OF LAW'

An underlying theme in jurisprudence is the notion that the concept of legality, known as the 'rule of law', provides at least part of the solution to the problem of arbitrary government.[4] On this view, the ideal of the 'rule of law' operates as an umbrella concept for legal-institutional mechanisms that protect the individual against the arbitrary power of the State. As aptly remarked by Owen Hood Phillips (1907-1986), who was emeritus professor of jurisprudence and public law at the University of Birmingham,

> Historically, the phrase [rule of law] was first used with reference to a belief in the existence of law possessing higher authority – whether divine or natural – than that of the law promulgated by human rulers which imposed limits on their powers. It was probably in this sense that Aristotle expressed the view that "the rule of law is preferable to that of any individual." Bracton, writing in the thirteenth century adopted the theory generally held in the Middle Ages that the world was governed by law, human or divine; and held that "the King himself ought not be subject to man but subject to God and to the law, because the law makes him king."[5]

The ultimate goal of the ideal of legality, known as the rule of law, is to provide "an umbrella concept for a number of legal and institutional instruments to protect citizens against the power of the State".[6] First coined by Plato and later refined by Aristotle, this concept was further elaborated by St Thomas Aquinas, who stated: "Once the government is established, the government of the kingdom must be so arranged that opportunity to tyrannize be removed. At the same time, his power should be so tempered that he cannot easily fall into tyranny".[7] That so being, writes Trevor Allan, a legal philosophy professor at the University of Cambridge, the rule of law is about the application of standards that "encompass traditional ideas about individual liberty and natural justice and, more generally, ideas about the requirements of justice and fairness in the relations between governors and governed".[8] According to him,

> The rule of law is both a political ideal and a constitutional doctrine. In English law, the rule of law expresses a general principle of constitutionalism, associated not only with procedural fairness and the impartial administration of law but also with ideas of human dignity and respect for persons.[9]

In a rule-of-law system, the basic rights of the individual must be protected by an independent judiciary with authority "to invalidate legislation if necessary".[10] As a result, the concept also encompasses an idea that "the law is to constitute a bulwark between governors and governed, shielding the individual from hostile discrimination on the part of those with political power".[11] As also stated by Professor Allan,

> In the mouth of a British constitutional lawyer, the term 'rule of law' seems to mean primarily a corpus of basic principles and values, which, together lend some stability and coherence to the legal order. It expresses his commitment to a scheme of ideas regarded as legally fundamental. They help to define the nature of the constitution, reflecting constitutional history and generating expectations about the conduct and character of modern government ... Allegiance to the 'rule of law' is not, therefore, a technical (or even 'lawyerly') commitment; it is necessarily allegiance

to a political philosophy — albeit a practical philosophy grounded in existing constitutional tradition.[12]

The same conception of the rule of law is embraced across the Western world. In continental Europe, the concept is traditionally associated with government that is "bound by the law in its dealings with citizens: its power is in other words limited by the individual rights of the people".[13] In Germany, the equivalent of the rule of law is called *Rechtsstaat* (*'State under the Law'*). First coined by Hanoverian jurists of the 19th century (R. von Mohl, E. Brandes, A.W. Rehberg and F.C. Dahlmann), in the words of the late German constitutional law professor, Ernst-Wolfgang Böckenförde (1930-2019):

> Rechtsstaat means primarily recognition of the fundamental rights such as civil liberty (protection of personal freedom, freedom of belief and conscience, freedom of the press, freedom of movement, freedom of contract, and freedom of occupation), equality before the law, and the guarantee of (acquired) property.[14]

However, the contemporary debate in the English-speaking world surrounding the meaning of the rule of law tends to start with the views of Albert Venn Dicey (1835-1922), a 19th-century English jurist and constitutional theorist. Dicey first published his *The Law of the Constitution*, based on lectures he delivered as Vinerian Professor of English Constitutional Law at Oxford, in 1885. A large part of the book is devoted to an exposition of the rule of law, "and this had a profound influence among those who think and write about the constitution, as well as those who work it".[15] Dicey's definition of the rule of law encompasses three distinct though kindred conceptions:

> (1) The absence of arbitrary power. No person is above the law. Nobody is punishable except for a clear breach of law, established in the ordinary parliamentary manner and before the ordinary courts.

> (2) Equality before the law. Every person, whatever such person's

rank or condition, is subject to the ordinary law and the jurisdiction of the ordinary courts.

(3) The general principles of the Constitution – especially the basic rights of the individual, such as freedom of speech and association, are to be recognised and enforced by the courts.[16]

Since Dicey's contributions, the concept of the rule of law has perennially been described as something that seeks to protect the citizen against unpredictable and arbitrary interferences with their personal freedoms. In this context, the security which everyone must enjoy for personal freedom is regarded as a fundamental legal right, because, as Dicey himself put it, "personal freedom does not really depend upon or originate in any general proposition contained in any written document".[17] This ideal of legality requires a delineation of governmental actions so that power is exercised in accordance with clear and generally applicable rules of law, which are clear, stable, enacted in advance, and enforced by an independent judiciary.

The requirement that laws must be "stable" is central to understanding the debate on the merits and demerits of mandatory vaccination rules. If legal rules were to change constantly – for example, who can and cannot have a certain vaccine – people would lose confidence in the ability of the legal system to prevent arbitrary decision-making by the authorities. In this context, it is broadly understood that legal stability is one of the most essential elements for the realisation of the rule of law. Legal stability is necessary for citizens to know the general rules that govern their lives. By contrast, constant changes in legal directions, especially when these are done by means of executive orders and without a proper parliamentary scrutiny, make it extremely hard, if not impossible, for anyone to plan his or her life according to predicable legal standards. Bearing this important fact in mind, the 19th-century French political theorist and constitutional lawyer, Benjamin Constant, stated:

> It is the imprudent multiplication of laws which in some periods has thrown discredit upon the most noble of things, on liberty itself, and made men seek refuge in the most miserable and lowest of them, servitude.[18]

In forestalling the imposition of ever-changing health orders on people – whether they concern face-masking, mandatory vaccination, and social distancing, among others – the 'rule of law' thus effectively shields people from efforts "to destroy, enslave, or … impoverish" them.[19] Above all, the concept of legality known as the 'rule of law' encompasses "traditional ideas about individual liberty and natural justice and, more generally, ideas about the requirements of justice and fairness in the relations between governors and governed".[20] Accordingly, laws must limit, control, and guide the exercise of discretionary power. As Professor Allan properly reminds us,

> It would be foolish to ignore or deny the real threat to liberty that such discretionary powers present; they leave the citizen at the mercy of the judgement of public officials, who may have little incentive to allow even reasonable objections to thwart their pursuit of their own policy agendas. There is a danger of oppression or unfairness, even when officials are well intentioned and act in good faith in (what they deem) the public interest".[21]

In this sense, American law professor Mortimer Sellers comments that, as the *imperium legis*, the rule of law effectively "requires of us that we remove the will of public officials as much as possible from the administration of justice in society".[22] According to him,

> Advocates of rule by law sometimes undermine the rule of law by legitimating the enactments of tyrants. Positive laws may sometimes be an advance on otherwise unregulated tyranny. Promulgations and the other virtues of legal formalism often advance the empire of laws. But they are only secondary and contingent requirements of the rule of law, not the thing itself.[23]

Ultimately, writes Robin Charlow, in his contribution for a book edited some years ago by the President of the American Bar

Association:

> The goal of the rule of law is to prevent the accretion of broad power in particular individuals or groups of rulers who might be tempted to govern according to their own autocratic policies rather than in the interests of the people generally. Rule of law is rule by pre-set standards, as contrasted with arbitrary and unpredictable rule according to the changing whims of men ... Freedom and justice [is] to be secured by public, fixed, durable laws, uniformly applied.[24]

Unfortunately, the classical understanding of the 'rule of law' is gradually becoming obsolete and overturned by "progressive" ideas that incorporate a myriad of statist considerations which seriously disregard the liberal-democratic legal traditions upon which Australia was once founded. Consequently, the level of general confidence in this ideal of legality is demonstrably declining, although, eventually, wrote the late Philip Selznick, the rule of law can only be preserved by means of

> a culture of lawfulness, that is, of routine respect, self-restraint, and deference ... Furthermore, the 'rule of law' requires public confidence in its premises as well as in its virtues. The premises include a dim but powerful understanding that positive law is always subject to correlation by standards of truth and justice. In a rule-of-law culture, positive law does not have the last word.[25]

The realisation of the rule of law therefore, depends "as much on characteristics of society as of the law, and on their interactions".[26] This ideal of legality is not just a matter of detailed legal-institutional design but, primarily, an "interconnected cluster of values" that can be pursued in a variety of legal-institutional ways.[27] Indeed, the fact it has often "thrived best where it was least designed"[28] appears to indicate that the realisation of the rule of law is not just about legal-institutional design but also social-cultural outcomes.[29] This is so because this ideal of legality cannot be disassociated from the moral tradition of the community. Hence, as so eloquently stated by Friedrich A. Hayek in *The Constitution of Liberty* (1960):

> From the fact that the 'rule of law' is a limitation upon all legis-
> lation, it follows that it cannot itself be a law in the same sense as
> the laws passed by the legislator ... The 'rule of law' is therefore
> not a rule of the law, but a rule concerning what the law ought to
> be, a meta-legal doctrine or a political ideal. It will be effective
> only in so far as the legislator feels bound by it. In a democracy,
> this means that it will not prevail unless it forms part of the moral
> tradition of the community, a common ideal shared and unques-
> tionably accepted by the majority. It is this fact that makes so very
> ominous the persistent attacks on the principle of the 'rule of law'
> ... But if it is represented as an impracticable and even undesirable
> ideal and people cease to strive for its realization, it will rapidly
> disappear. Such a society will quickly relapse into a state of arbi-
> trary tyranny.[30]

It is, therefore, imperative to consider that law is not always the
primary element of political legitimisation.[31] Sometimes there are
other and more culturally acceptable ways to legitimise power
rather than via legal means. Through charismatic leadership, for
example, power is not primarily legitimised by legal-institutional
mechanisms but instead via the devotion to the generally
perceived "exceptional sanctity, heroism, or exemplary character
of an individual person, and of the normative patterns or order
revealed or ordained by him".[32] This state of affairs results in
the phenomenon of 'charismatic leadership' being more socially
accepted as a more valid form of legitimisation of power than
constitutionalism. As Sir Ivor Jennings KBE QC FBA, a British
lawyer and legal academic who served as the Vice-Chancellor of
the University of Cambridge, properly observed:

> If it is believed that the individual finds his greatest happiness,
> or best develops his soul, in a strong and powerful State, and that
> government implies... the unity of the [community] behind a wise
> and beneficent leader, the rule of law is a pernicious doctrine.[33]

What gives real life to the rule of law lies in the social environment,
which, according to Sir Lawrence Friedman, "is constantly at

work on the law – destroying here, renewing there; invigorating here, deadening there; choosing what parts of law will operate, which parts will not; what substitutes, detours, and bypasses will spring up; what changes will take place".[34] We may, therefore, conclude that the elements that lead to the realisation of the rule of law simply cannot operate more effectively when "political leaders do not fear citizen mobilization when fundamental rules of the game are violated".[35] As the American political scientist and emeritus professor, Noel B. Reynolds, asserted:

> The rule of law does poorly in cultures where it is not the funda-
> mental expectation that a people has of its government... If peo-
> ple do not expect the rule of law and insist on it when officials
> move to compromise its effect, it is soon corrupted and replaced
> by rule of will. Rule of law seems to require this virtue of any
> populace that will enjoy its benefits.[36]

Central to the concept of the rule of law is also the conviction that a proper application of the doctrine of separation of powers constitutes "a critical aspect of every system of government which hopes to combine efficiency and the greatest possible exercise of personal freedom".[37] The idea rests on the view that when power becomes too concentrated in the hands of a few, then the risk of oppression naturally increases. Washington University law professor Brian Z. Tamanaha comments on the rationale for separating the powers of the State according to the 'rule of law':

> *Freedom is enhanced when the powers of the government are di-*
> *vided into separate compartments — typically legislative, execu-*
> *tive, and judicial (horizontal division), and sometimes municipal,*
> *state or regional, and national (vertical division) ... This division*
> *of powers promotes liberty by preventing the accumulation of to-*
> *tal power in any single institution, setting up a form of competi-*
> *tive interdependence within the government.*[38]

The dilution of executive and legislative separation in the Westminster system is now having a number of disastrous implications, each of which law professor Suri Ratnapala views as being key flaws in the Australian constitutional scheme. To make it worse, he continues, "[i]n Australia, the High Court, despite having full judicial power has declined to impose on Parliament any significant constraint on its competence to delegate its legislative power to the executive".[39] Pointing to decisions such as *Victorian Stevedoring & General Contracting Co Ltd v Dignan*,[40] Ratnapala laments that the Court has chosen to not "draw the line in the sand against excessive delegation", despite functional "parliamentary democracies rely[ing] heavily on judicial oversight of executive action".[41]

It has long been held that accountable government requires an effective separation of legislative, executive, and judicial powers. Accountability is central to democratic, representative government, but this is not possible if all power is concentrated in the hands of a few. However, the design and operation of our current parliamentary system is not about distributing institutional powers, thus making accountability difficult to achieve. In Australia, the Crown no longer has any power to intervene in the political process, "dormant" or otherwise. The Head of State is constitutionally bound by the Australia Acts to act on the Premier's commands.

In the words of Sir Ivor Jennings, "All power is likely to be abused unless it is adequately checked". This is, it must be stressed, a problem of unchecked power, and here we are reminded of Lord Acton's warning that, "Power tends to corrupt and absolute power corrupts absolutely'.[42] Charles-Louis de Secondat, Baron de La Brède et de Montesquieu, generally referred to as Montesquieu, was a French judge, historian, and political philosopher. To restrain the abuse of power, he explained: "It is necessary from the disposition of things that power should be a check to power". He also argued that there would be no protection against tyranny if the legislative power is not separate from the executive. Thus,

Montesquieu concluded:

> When the legislative and executive powers are united in the same person, or in the same body of magistrates, there can be no liberty; because apprehensions may arise, lest the same monarch or senate should enact tyrannical laws, to execute them in a tyrannical manner.

But it might be correctly stated that in Westminster systems there is no proper separation of executive and legislative powers. According to law professor Nicholas Aroney,

> Under contemporary conditions of parliamentary government, there is a tendency for both executive and legislative power to be concentrated effectively in a very small group of senior ministers, dominated by the prime minister or premier.[43]

The Westminster system of executive-parliament lies at the very heart of Australia's present constitutional crisis at all levels of Government. As noted by Martyn Webb, who was Emeritus Professor of Geography at the University of Western Australia, "this is a system of government which, by giving far too much power to the executive, corrupts democracy, reducing it to little more than a period right to vote".[44] The rise to dominance of the authoritarian leader in Australia is therefore, a confirmation of the massive shift of power away from parliament, or the legislative arm of government, to the executive or cabinet. This process not only effectively allows the Premier and his cabinet to arbitrarily decide on legislative measures but also to intervene on every single aspect of our lives. In the next chapter, we will explain how the concentration of powers in the hands of a few politicians has facilitated the enactment of emergency powers that paves the way for arbitrary government and the undermining of basic rights of the individual.

3

THE USE OF EMERGENCY POWERS

The deep unease and fear that saturate Australia's society have created a population disposed to governments whose insatiable thirst for power and control leads to authoritarian measures. To avoid the growing concern of human rights violations and outright suppression of the constitutional order, the political establishment has learned about the importance of manipulating public perceptions to win support of what normally would be rejected as oppressive and undemocratic measures. Significantly, the political class has not acted alone, relying on so-called "chief health advisers" who then become the *de facto* rulers over the people as the establishment's effective enablers.

Providing discretionary directions, these advisers are perfectly positioned to act as the mastermind behind most of the government's extra-constitutional schemes. Part of such a master plan, of course, involves dismantling the rule of law. Paradoxically, the nation's political class has managed to undermine the rule of law through legal means. The success at sustaining legitimacy to arbitrary rule and maintaining a façade of legality arises out of a narrow positivistic justification used to shroud otherwise unconstitutional exercises of power that violate the most elementary principles of the rule of law.

While these political rulers claim to be "saving" lives, they have set in motion the gradual accumulation of power in the hands of a few individuals, thus solidifying their extensive power primarily through the creation of legal loopholes that hide the invalidity of unconstitutional measures through a legalistic veneer. To begin, the institution of emergency powers which authorise governments to rule by executive orders comprise measures that engender an unfair system and which do not guarantee the equality of everyone before the law, and the appropriate checks to executive government.

In his classic text, *The Spirit of Laws*, Montesquieu crystallises the more relevant aspects of despotism: "In despotic government, one alone … draws everything along by his will and his caprices".[45] And later: "the principle of despotic government [is]… fear".[46] One way that despotic government is manifesting itself in Australia is through the expanding volume of legislative discretions given to the executive, which, in the words of Suri Ratnapala, is "a bit like entrusting the sheep to the wolf".[47] According to him,

> The rule against the delegation of wide law making power to the executive is a major component of the classical doctrine of separation of powers. When officials can both legislate and execute their legislation, they have the potential to place themselves above the law, for the 'law' is what they command.[48]

Without the protection of civil liberties, a country cannot call itself a true democracy. To avoid the growing concern of outright suppression of basic human rights, the ruling oligarchy has learned about the necessity of manipulating public perceptions to win support of what normally would be rejected as unconstitutional measures. Government propaganda, which is disseminated by the mainstream media, has been deeply successful in justifying these measures, thus making the media an effective means of censoring anti-establishment messages. Without an alternative view, of course, the public tend to view reports of human rights violations merely as "excesses" or "collateral damage" – the price to fight a "deadly virus".

The experience of contemporary Australia vividly exemplifies a disguised form of authoritarianism under the façade of temporary measures to combat an alleged health crisis. Rather than openly violating the constitutional order, governmental accountability is dangerously weakened by insulating the political ruler from scrutiny and a functioning system of checks and balances.

An example of a particularly odious attempt at denigrating Australia's democratic institutions is the adoption by the Victorian Parliament of its controversial *Public Health and Wellbeing Amendment (Pandemic Management) Bill* 2021 which gives the Premier unprecedented power to rule by decree without having to seek the prior approval of Parliament.[49] The legislation even allows differentiation between people on the ground of their vaccine status, while claiming that the legislation is consistent with Victoria's Charter of Rights. The Minister of Health would be able to make health orders under this radical anti-democratic legislation to better fight the COVID-19 pandemic and future pandemics.

The danger is that, when governments change as might happen eventually, these odious laws will remain on the statute book. It is uncertain that a new government would have the capacity or the will to repeal these laws. Victoria's opposition leader, Matthew Guy, has given an "absolute guarantee" that the Liberal Party, when it comes to power, will repeal this legislation. History will reveal whether this promise is mere puff or a genuine attempt at restoring parliamentary democracy in Victoria, which respects the application of the rule of law.

Not surprisingly, demonstrations against this draconian legislation turned violent when construction workers marched in Melbourne on Saturday, 6 November 2021. On that day, thousands of protesters assembled to protest the vaccine mandates of the Victorian government and the unparalleled power grab which the legislation makes possible.

However, Australians usually do not protest even if the political class adopts laws which demean the rule of law. Why does the public permit this unabashed expansion of governmental power? Fear of death has become ingrained in the psyche of the Australian population. Importantly, the arbitrary use of power depends on maintaining public support through a clearly calculated media campaign that sustains an irrational level of public fear and anxiety. In consultation with carefully chosen, so-called health advisers, politicians can manipulate a significant sector of the media which then sensationalise COVID-19 cases and manipulate the masses. The carefully carried psychological campaign aims at instilling great fear in the general populace.

This recipe for despotic rule has re-ordered political and social manners in Australia, thus creating a culture of fear that perpetuates the willingness of citizens to surrender their basic legal rights in exchange for a false sense of security. As such, the average citizen becomes prone to cede these legal rights for a paternalistic government in exchange for more safety and protection. The legal-institutional structures which have well served to protect the citizen from external oppression – the *sine qua non* of democratic government – tend to disappear in the process. Without constitutional guarantees of the basic rights to freely associate, to freedom of speech, and to the inviolability of the person's bodily autonomy, democratic society shrivels under the threat of authoritarianism, the status quo actively contributing decisively to the undermining of the rule of law and inalienable rights of the individual.

Despite the alleged success in the "war" against a supposedly deadly virus, governments in Australia do not seem willing to terminate their emergency powers or decrease the use of health directives, hence the ongoing justification for the continuing use of such powers. Instead, the political establishment has capitalised on public fear and anxiety as a successful means of assuring the gradual consolidation of unchecked rule. This institutionalisation of fear allows the political establishment to control and immobilise civil society. In this context, the label "anti-vax" becomes an efficient means of silencing any opposition to the narrative of the status quo, thus undermining one of the primary pillars of democracy: freedom of speech. The 'anti-vax' slur operates via a form of 'contagion theory' whereby calling anyone a 'conspiracy theorist', or implying that they oppose all forms of vaccination, are Machiavellian attempts to silence rational debate and democratic dialogue.

In theory, the use of emergency powers by the ruling elites should be a temporary departure from constitutional rule, in which a political leader might need to rule by decree until the emergency ceases to exist. The Australian political establishment, however, may never intend these measures to be temporary, thus seeking to conveniently maintain its extraordinary powers indefinitely. As such, convincing the population of a perpetual state of emergency gives the ruling elite broad discretionary authority to govern at the margin of the democratic process, unconstrained by legal-institutional accountability.

Ultimately, the success of any authoritarian endeavour requires popular acquiescence. Convincing the population of a grave health emergency leads to less popular resistance and more political space in which to expand its arbitrary powers. If the political establishment can convince the people that a great public emergency exists, it faces less resistance to continue expanding its governmental power. In this context, the coronavirus phenomenon shows how easily the rule of law breaks down when an alleged threat taps into the population's deepest fears.

Surely, a government always reserves the right to enact emergency powers to protect the health of the people. Even international law recognises that during these extraordinary times, governments may suspend normal constitutional protections, except for inalienable non-derogable rights. When the political leader violates these inalienable rights, then he or she must be held accountable for transgressing the substantive norms associated with the rule of law. In these ways the political leader is automatically susceptible to the commitment of human rights violations that may eventually lead to charges of crimes against humanity.

The *Universal Declaration of Human Rights* openly recognises, in its Preamble, the critical role of the rule of law in preserving the inalienable rights of the individual, by stating:

> Whereas it is essential, if man is not to be compelled to have recourse, as a last resort, to rebellion against tyranny and oppression, that human rights should be protected by the rule of law.

Therefore, in the context of international human rights legislation, it is unquestionable that the nation's political establishment has violated an international definition of the rule of law which includes the lawful right of citizens to resist unconstitutional instances of arbitrary government. The lawful right to resist arbitrary government is certainly guaranteed by the *International Covenant on Civil and Political Rights* (ICCPR). Under its Article 19, "everyone shall have the right to freedom of expression". And as stated by Article 18 of the ICCPR, "everyone shall have the right to freedom of thought, conscience and religion".

We can only hope Australians will no longer tolerate any further abdication of their fundamental rights, as they finally wake up to the disguised efforts of the political establishment to ensconce itself in power. When this happens, of course, the extraordinary accumulation of unrestrained power by the ruling classes will no longer be justifiable as a legitimate measure, thus revealing a deliberate attempt to eliminate the rule of law via the expansion (and concentration) of such a power in the hands of an entrenched oligarchy.

4

THE UNCONSTITUTIONALITY OF VACCINE MANDATES

The assertion in our previous chapters that the 'rule of law' requires public confidence in its premises as well as in its virtues is apposite to a discussion of the constitutionality of mandatory vaccination rules in Australia. But, anticipating a discussion of this issue, it is first necessary to review the relationship of the 'rule of law' to the concept of 'constitutionalism' in Australia's constitutional framework.

Like the traditional view or perception of the 'rule of law', the concept of 'constitutionalism' implies a system of constitutional government that involves separation of powers and, accordingly, limitation of the state's arbitrary power. In this sense, it would be erroneous to employ the term 'constitutional government' with reference to arbitrary government, or an elected dictatorship. Commenting on 'constitutionalism', Professor Ratnapala states:

> A Constitution in the proper sense is a constitution of a partic-
> ular type. It limits the powers of rulers by subordinating them
> to enduring rules that they themselves cannot abrogate. Such a
> constitution is inextricably associated with the ideal of the 'rule
> of law', which seeks to ensure that people are not at the mercy of
> the momentary will of a ruler or a ruling group, but enjoy stability
> of life, liberty and property.[50]

The liberal legal tradition of 'constitutionalism', or 'constitutional government', laid the basis for representative democracy and the constitutional protection of citizens against arbitrary power. Under this tradition, to be under the law presupposes the existence of constitutional rules and principles serving as an effective check on government. As stated by Professor C.L. Ten:

> Constitutionalism and the 'rule of law' are related ideas about how the powers of government and of state officials are to be limited. The two ideas are sometimes equated. But constitutionalism usually refers to specific constitutional devices and procedures, such as the separation of powers between the legislature, the executive and the judiciary, the independence of the judiciary, due process or fair hearings for those charged with criminal offences, and respect for individual rights, which are partly constitutive of a liberal democratic system of government ... The requirements of constitutionalism are derived from a political morality which seeks to promote individual rights and freedoms, and not directly from values that are supposed to be implicit in the very idea of [positive] law itself.[51]

In this sense, it appears particularly relevant to consider that the requirements of constitutional government are directly associated with Australia's liberal-democratic traditions of government under the law, which seek to provide effective protection to individual rights and freedoms. As stated by Justice Gaudron in *Australian Capital Television Ltd v Commonwealth*, "the notion of a free society governed in accordance with the principles of representative parliamentary democracy may entail freedom of movement, freedom of association and ... freedom of speech generally".[52]

Furthermore, it is entirely reasonable to assume that any legislative command which directly violates these fundamental freedoms is not law properly so called. In *Nationwide News Pty Ltd v Wills*, Justice Brennan stated: "Where a representative democracy is constitutionally entrenched, it carries with it those legal incidents which are essential to the effective maintenance of government".[53] In other words, once it is judicially recognised that a system of representative democracy is constitutionally prescribed, then the preservation of these fundamental rights and freedoms is "essential to sustain it as firmly entrenched in the Constitution as the system of government which the Constitution explicitly ordains".[54]

In this sense, it is self-evident that Australians are endowed with important constitutional protections which are directly derived from the notion espoused by the High Court that we are a free society governed in accordance with the principles of democratic, parliamentary government. If this is so, a failure to protect this essential aspect of our constitutional framework would transform the Constitution into a less reliable document when it comes to restricting arbitrary power and ensuring the operation of constitutional government. In this context, Giovanni Sartori, an Italian political scientist, would accurately describe such a constitution as no more than a "façade".[55]

The Australian Constitution must be interpreted in a manner that promotes its purposes, values, and principles, advancing the rule of law and the fundamental rights of the citizen. To implement the 'rule of law' and 'constitutionalism', the Australian Constitution expressly limits the exercise of governmental powers. In drafting the Constitution, the framers deliberately sought to design an instrument of government intended to distribute and limit the powers of the State. This distribution of, and limitation upon, governmental powers was intentionally chosen because of the proper understanding that unrestrained power is always inimical to the achievement of human freedom and happiness. Anthony Murray Gleeson, a former Chief Justice of the High Court, describes the Constitution's feature of express limitation on governmental powers as follows:

> ... no one is above the law. Thus government officials must exer-

cise their powers according to law. If they do not then, in the last resort, the High Court may order them to do so. The Constitution ... itself declares that the government must obey the law, and gives the High Court the jurisdiction to compel such obedience. That jurisdiction cannot be removed or modified except by constitutional amendment. Parliament, if acting within the limits of the powers assigned to it by the Constitution, may change the law. But the executive government must obey the law.[56]

Accordingly, the Constitution allocates the areas of legislative power to the Commonwealth primarily in sections 51 and 52, with these powers being variously exclusive or concurrent with the Australian States. The Constitution was amended in a referendum in 1946 to include section 51(xxiiiA), which stipulates that the Commonwealth parliament, among others, can make laws with respect to:

The provision of ... pharmaceutical, sickness and hospital benefits, medical and dental services (but not so as to authorize any form of civil conscription), benefits to students and family allowances.

This provision allows for the granting of various services by the federal government but not to the extent of authorising any form of civil conscription.[57] Thus, medical practitioners may not be compelled by the Federal government to provide mandatory services, for example, vaccinations. However, an *AAP FactCheck* article which analyses this constitutional provision concludes that, "While the Australian Constitution may prevent the federal government from forcing medical practitioners to provide services – such as administering COVID-19 vaccines – it does not expressly bar the government from introducing vaccination requirements."[58]

According to constitutional law commentators, contacted by AAP FactCheck, any claim that section 51(xxiiiA) of the Constitution bans mandatory vaccinations is "pseudo-legal nonsense" and "far-fetched", because the section does "not grant people individual "rights"; it merely "prevents the federal government from forcing people to do work as doctors and dentists." A commentator, Luke Beck, indicated that, "There's nothing in the constitution that would prevent a law making COVID vaccination mandatory." Similarly, Professor George Williams told AAP FactCheck that section 51(xxiiiA) "would not prevent the Commonwealth from requiring citizens to be vaccinated." He stated that the section could be relied upon to prevent the Commonwealth, but not the States, from compelling medical practitioners to take part in mass vaccination programs.

These academic views have been supported in a judgment rendered by Justice Robert Beech-Jones, on 15 October 2021, in the New South Wales Supreme Court. Justice Beech-Jones is the State's Chief Judge at common law. He opined in *Kassam v Hazzard; Henry v Hazzard*[59] that the term 'civil conscription' in section 51(xxiiiA) of the Constitution was "directed to compulsory service in the *provision* of medical services as opposed to the acquisition of services such as vaccinations by a patient." In *Kassam*, the plaintiffs challenged the New South Wales public health orders requiring vaccination in certain circumstances on the ground that the legislation infringed section 51(xxiiiA) of the Constitution. The Court, dismissing the plaintiffs' challenges, also noted that section 51(xxiiiA) "is directed to the legislative power of the Commonwealth not the states."[60]

Nevertheless, the implementation of mandatory COVID-19 vaccination sits uncomfortably with the High Court's jurisprudence. This is because section 51(xxiiiA), while it prohibits civil conscription, does not limit the right of medical practitioners to offer vaccination services to their patients, who want to avail themselves of these services. In that case, the provision of vaccination services is based on the contractual relationship between doctors and patients. There are thus two constitutional challenges to overcome when attempting to interpret section 51(xxiiiA) as prohibiting mandatory vaccinations: (i) the construction of the section as granting a constitutional right to patients to refuse vaccinations, and (ii) the applicability of the section to the States.

The first challenge relates to the construction of section 51(xxiiiA) as giving a constitutional right to individuals to refuse vaccination. If section 51(xxiiiA) were to be interpreted as allowing mandatory vaccination, then the contractual relationship between doctor and patients would be effectively abolished because the patients' ability to enter a contract for the receipt of vaccination services would be non-existent. Yet, Justice Kirby opined in 2009, in *Wong v Commonwealth; Selim v Professional Services Review Committee*,[61] that the purpose of prohibiting the conscription in section 51(xxiiiA) was to ensure that the relationship between medical practitioner and patient was governed by contract where that is the intention of the parties. For him the test whether civil conscription has been imposed is "whether the impugned regulation, by its details and burdens, intrudes impermissibly into the private consensual arrangements between the providers of medical and dental services and the individual recipients of such services."[62]

Justice Kirby's point reveals that compulsory vaccination destroys the contractual relationship between doctors and patients and, therefore, it imposes an impermissible obligation on people to accept a medical procedure which they can refuse on constitutional grounds. Section 51(xxiiiA) could thus also be regarded as an implied constitutional right of individual patients to refuse vaccinations.

The concept of "civil conscription" was first considered by the High Court in 1949 in *British Medical Association v Commonwealth*.[63] The Court ruled that requiring doctors to comply with professional standards to receive Medicare payments did not amount to civil conscription. But the Court also relevantly decided that legislation which required that medical practitioners use a particular Commonwealth prescription form as part of a scheme to provide pharmaceutical benefits was invalid as a form of civil conscription. In the opinion of Chief Justice Latham, civil conscription included not only legal compulsion to engage in specific conduct, but also the imposition of a duty to perform work in a particular way. Justice Williams, in his judgment, stated that

> the expression **invalidates all legislation** which **compels medical practitioners or dentists to provide any form of medical service**" (emphasis added).[64]

In 2009, in *Wong v Commonwealth; Selim v Professional Services Review Committee,*[65] Chief Justice French and Justice Gummow held that civil conscription is a "compulsion or coercion in the legal and practical sense, to carry out work or provide [medical] services".[66] In summary, the 'no conscription' requirement to be found in that constitutional provision amounts to an explicit limitation on mandating the provision of medical services, for example compulsory vaccination, which remains governed by the contractual relationship between patients and doctors.

Hence, if the medical profession were directed by the government to mandatorily vaccinate people, such direction would constitute an unconstitutional civil conscription. Such direction would interfere with the relationship between the doctor and the patient – a relationship which is based on contract and trust. Of course, medical doctors who freely perform their medical service do not create conscription. However, as Justice Webb explicitly mentioned:

> When Parliament comes between patient and doctor and makes the lawful continuance of their relationship as such depend upon

a condition, enforceable by fine, that the doctor shall render the patient a special service, unless that service is waived by the patient, it creates a situation that amounts to a form of civil conscription. [67]

Justice Webb's statement also indicates that, even if the doctor were compelled to provide a service, the patient would have the right to waive that service. In other words, no citizen shall be in any way coerced into any medical treatment whatsoever, including vaccination. A medical treatment which is imposed upon a person without his or her informed consent is a trespass upon that person. In *Bowater v Rowley Regis Corp*, Lord Justice Scott explained that consent to treatment, including vaccination, is needed to proceed with the treatment:

> … a man cannot be said to be truly 'willing' unless he is in a position to choose freely, and freedom of choice predicates, not only full knowledge of the circumstances on which the exercise of choice is conditioned, so that he may be able to choose wisely, but in the absence from his mind of any feeling of restraint so that nothing shall interfere with the freedom of his will.[68]

The second challenge relates to the applicability of section 51(xxiiiA) to the Australian States: although a State government can institute its own public health orders, any component of such order cannot impermissibly intrude into any matter which may be regarded as coming within the sole legislative authority of the Commonwealth Parliament. When this occurs, of course, the applicant State must make application to the Commonwealth to enact that specific component of the health order on behalf of the State. Accordingly, the issue of vaccine mandates is not whether an Australian State can issue a public health order, but rather whether such State is constitutionally authorised to issue a public health order, which unreasonably intrudes into a matter that comes within the sole purview of the Commonwealth.

Mr John Lawrence Duval, a concerned citizen, raised this

important argument in an email message of 11 November 2021 addressed to the federal Attorney-General. Duval relevantly argued that, "although a State Government has the right to institute public health orders, if any component of such health order intrudes into that which is the sole purview of the Commonwealth, then the State must make application to the Commonwealth for the Commonwealth to enact that particular component on behalf of the State."[69] In his email communication, Mr Duval explains that in the State where he resides, Victoria, the government has recently adopted a 'no jab, no job' rule, which effectively prevents people from earning a living unless he or she is vaccinated with a COVID-19 vaccine. Consequently, citizens who reside in Victoria now suffer from a significant disadvantage relative to most Australians who are residing in another State: the former are *not* allowed to work if *not* vaccinated, the latter are allowed; the former are *not* allowed to supplement their unemployment benefits with part time income, the latter are allowed.

The "no jab, no job" health order of the Victorian government is, of course, an egregious violation of a right which is fundamentally attached to 'citizenship'. Although the Commonwealth Constitution does not say anything about 'citizenship', section 51(xix) gives legislative power to the Commonwealth Parliament to make laws with respect to "Naturalization and aliens". At present, Victoria is the only State with a 'no jab, no job' health order. This means that Australian citizens are treated differently depending on the State they live in. Duval argued that this order is invalid because "the right to earn a living is fundamentally attached to citizenship rather than one's place of residence, and thus that the State Government of Victoria must apply to the Commonwealth Government to implement such prohibition on its behalf, which it has not done."

In this context, Article 6(1) of the International Covenant on Economic, Social and Cultural Rights, which entered into force on 3 January 1976, stipulates that, "The States Parties to the present Covenant recognize the right to work, which includes the right of everyone to the opportunity to gain his living by work which he freely chooses or accepts, and will take appropriate steps to safeguard this right." Of course, a request, that the Commonwealth adopt a 'no jab, no job' health order on behalf of the State, would activate the applicability of section 51(xxiiiA) of the Constitution. Indeed, as this provision explicitly prohibits the imposition of civil conscriptions by means of coercive vaccine mandates, especially if they were to affect the contractual relationship between doctors and patients, the Commonwealth is constitutionally prevented from assisting the States in the implementation of any such measures that would result in a form of enforced medical conscription.

Importantly, the jurisprudence of the High Court indicates that the prohibition of civil conscription must be construed widely to invalidate any law requiring such conscription expressly or by practical implication. In other words, no law in Australia can impose limitations on the rights of citizens that directly or indirectly amount to a form of civil conscription. If governments cannot constitutionally force everyone to be vaccinated, they certainly cannot indirectly create a situation whereby everybody would be forced to take the vaccine. This point is also addressed in a comment of Justice Webb in *British Medical Association v Commonwealth*:

> If Parliament cannot lawfully do this directly by legal means **it cannot lawfully do it indirectly** by creating a situation, as distinct from merely taking advantage of one, in which the individual is left no real choice but compliance" (emphasis added).[70]

Furthermore, compulsory vaccination adversely affects the democratic principle of equality before the law. If unvaccinated

Australians were to face serious restrictions of rights and freedoms – as suggested by medical officers and the Prime Minister – these restrictions would violate the democratic principle of equality before the law. Accordingly, in *Leeth v Commonwealth*,[71] Justice Deane and Justice Toohey referred to the Preamble to the Constitution to support their view that the principle of equality is embedded impliedly in the Constitution. They argued that "the essential or underlying theoretical equality of all persons under the law and before the courts is and has been a fundamental and generally beneficial doctrine of the common law and a basic prescript of the administration of justice under our system of government."[72]

The deliberate exclusion of unvaccinated Australians from participation in certain activities discriminates against them on the ground of vaccine status. Of course, vaccine status is not one of the accepted grounds in any anti-discrimination legislation and, therefore, it would be possible for governments to defeat a claim that compulsory vaccination violates the anti-discrimination principle. However, reliance on vaccine status would still create an apartheid-type situation since benefits would be conferred and burdens imposed on this ground. But, more importantly, the making of coercive statements to force people to get vaccinated would effectively amount to an indirect form of mandatory vaccination, the constitutionality of which is doubtful at best. Indeed, from a constitutional point of view, the jurisprudence of the High Court indicates that what cannot be done directly, cannot be achieved indirectly without violating section 51 of the Constitution.

It is also worth approaching the matter from the perspective of the dignity and privacy of individuals. Governments should avoid relying on the *parens patriae* doctrine according to which government will decide what is good for people: it would be a textbook example of the operation of the Nanny State that removes any sense of individual responsibility and human dignity. There is seriously a danger of excessive state paternalism when citizens are not allowed to make personal decisions about their own medical treatment, including the decision of whether to take a COVID-19 vaccine. This was highlighted in *Airdale National Health Service Trust v Bland*, when Lord Justice Mustill expounded on this danger with the following clarity:

> If the patient is capable of making a decision on whether to permit treatment and decides not to permit it his choice must be obeyed, even if on any objective view it is contrary to his best interests. A doctor has no right to proceed in the face of objection, even it if is plain to all, including the patient, that adverse consequences and even death will or may ensue.[73]

In fact, the approach taken by the Australian authorities violates international human rights law; it certainly contradicts the United Nations Universal Declaration of Human Rights. Elaborated under the auspices of Eleanor Roosevelt and her Commission, when she summed up the attitude of the framers, Roosevelt explained that this historical piece of international legislation was based on the expectation that everyone must have freedom in which to individually develop their "full stature and through common effort to raise the level of human dignity".[74]

Furthermore, the right of an individual to refuse vaccination is also supported by the *Nuremberg Code* – an ethics code – relied upon during the Nazi doctors' trials in Nuremberg. This Code has as its first principle the willingness and informed consent by the individual to receive medical treatment or to participate in an experiment. Recently, however, it has been argued in an AAP FactCheck that an attempt "to apply the code to COVID-19 vaccines is incorrect and misleading."[75] It notes that the Nuremberg Code only addresses human medical experimentation and does not apply to "approved vaccines". However, the FastCheck analysis turns on the fact that COVID-19 vaccines do not involve human experimentation, but instead have been approved – in Australia by the Therapeutic Goods Administration – for emergency use.

It is precisely the experimental nature of the COVID-19 vaccines and the widespread disagreement about the capacity of vaccines to provide protection against the virus that is responsible for the lack of confidence in their effectiveness. Indeed, in a climate of uncertainty, characterised by a demonstrable lack of confidence, as is amply demonstrated by the vaccine hesitancy in Australia, a programme of mandatory vaccination cannot be regarded as consensual. The unvaccinated, in relying on health implications for the purpose of refusing the vaccine, may thus ironically invoke the same argument used by proponents of vaccinations, who also rely on health grounds to promote the vaccine.

Hence, people's refusal to be vaccinated may be based on the ground that the COVID-19 vaccines are still experimental and their long-term effects and safety on its recipients are unknown. Indeed, the 'rule of law' would be undermined if mandatory vaccination were mandated in circumstances where constant government changes undermine the confidence of people in the efficient administration of the vaccine roll-out and the effectiveness of the vaccines. In fact, latest research confirms that these vaccines are not being able even to stop the spread of COVID-19. In other words, those who are vaccinated can still catch and transmit COVID-19. As evidence of the inefficacy of these vaccines, in a recent study supported by Centers for Disease and Prevention contracts, members of the Upper Midwest Regional Accelerator for Genomic Surveillance founded by the Rockefeller Foundation, concluded that vaccinated people can still catch and transmit COVID-19 and, once infected, the vaccinated are as likely to infect others as the unvaccinated.[76]

Nevertheless, Australian chief medical officers and their political handlers have embarked on a campaign to cajole people to vaccinate and attempted to rehabilitate the AstraZeneca vaccine as a suitable COVID-19 jab. The debate on the suitability of the AstraZeneca vaccine provides a good explanation for the demonstrable lack of confidence in the effectiveness of COVID-19 vaccines in Australia. The AstraZeneca vaccine lost much of its reputational shine when media disclosed that several deaths from blood clots with low blood platelets occurred after the deceased had been vaccinated with this vaccine. This blood clotting event involves a thrombosis with thrombocytopenia syndrome (TTS). The campaigners point out that the risk of blood clotting is only one out of 250,000 AstraZeneca jabs, whereas it is one out of 1,000 for women of child-bearing age who take the contraceptive pill. Thus, the rate of blood clotting from AstraZeneca compares favourably with the rate of blood clotting from the contraceptive pill. Professor Adam Taylor concludes that:

> With this in mind, it's worth remembering that while there is a small risk of clotting in some individuals who take the AstraZeneca vaccine, this clotting risk is much less than with many other things, including contraceptive pills – and significantly less than the risk of clotting after a COVID-19 infection.[77]

The question should be asked why people distrust AstraZeneca but not the contraceptive pill. An answer may be that many people, especially seniors, have come to believe that there is a more suitable, and possibly better vaccine available, namely Pfizer and Moderna. Although these vaccines, like any other vaccines, also have side effects, they did not initially seem to engender the blood clotting problems of the AstraZeneca vaccine. More importantly, a comparison between the blood clotting side effects of these novel vaccines and the contraceptive pill involves the making of a logical error. The error lies in comparing two treatments which are not comparable: one is a vaccine, the other is a pill, used for entirely different purposes. But in the case of vaccines, since they are used for the same purpose of inoculating people against the COVID-19 virus, it is possible to compare the performance of the three available vaccines with each other. Surely, the lack of confidence would not exist if the AstraZeneca vaccine were the only available vaccine on the market.

Hence, many people regard Pfizer as the gold standard in the COVID-19 jungle. Nevertheless, latest studies have revealed that the Pfizer vaccine actually carries the same risks of blood clouts as AstraZeneca vaccines.[78] Furthermore, Rocco Loiacono reports in an article in *The Spectator* that, "Data from the Israeli Minister of Health released on July 22 declared that the effectiveness of the Pfizer ... vaccine at preventing COVID-19 has plummeted from 90 percent to only 39 percent, coinciding with the spread of the Delta variant in the country."[79]

One of the most frustrating things surrounding the contentious vaccine debate is the existence of many different and inconsistent opinions and advice. Michael DiMarco, in an article in *The Spectator* correctly describes this frustration: "One of the great ironies of the COVID-19 pandemic is how consistent Western governments have been at providing inconsistent health advice." It is thus the predictability of unpredictability that is ruining the daily lives of people in Australia!

A person may be told by one specialist doctor that AstraZeneca is a potentially unsafe vaccine, compared with the Pfizer or Moderna vaccines. Other professionals may point to the negligible risk of taking the AstraZeneca jab compared with its immense potential benefits. Clearly, if the medical advice given is not consistently conveyed by the medical fraternity, it is no wonder that people lose confidence in the effectiveness of these vaccines and exhibit vaccine hesitancy. Also, it does not help that the shambolic rollout of the vaccines in Australia, especially in the first half of 2021 when Pfizer was not available for people over the age of 60, is a textbook example of how it should not be done. The damage caused by this lack of confidence to the 'rule of law' is palpable and results in it losing its characteristic of stability.

This lack of confidence is exacerbated when one considers the standards that vaccines should exhibit but fail to meet. There are at least five medical requirements that need to be met: (i) the vaccine must result in a measurable reduction in the number of sick people afflicted with the COVID-19 virus, (ii) the vaccine must be capable of protecting recipients for a significant time, thereby possibly avoiding booster shots, (iii) the vaccine should have few negative side effects, (iv) the vaccine must be effective against newer variants of the virus, and (v) the vaccine must substantially reduce transmission rates. There are four logistical requirements: (i) a low cost to produce the vaccine, (ii) the vaccine can be produced quickly on the required scale, (iii) the vaccine can be efficiently distributed, and (iv) it is easy to administer. Perhaps the most important, and final, requirement is that the public, medical professionals, and politicians confidently trust the vaccine.

Obviously, the vaccines on offer do not meet this final requirement of trust. Although 'trust' is often based on a misperception, a rational discussion just might save the reputation of the vaccination campaign. But right now, even members of the medical fraternity are bewildered and do not know what to think; they disagree with regards to the advice they can give to their patients. Even so, the federal government has recently announced that, "through continued engagement with Pfizer-BioNTech, the Government has secured 60 million doses in 2022, and 25 million doses in 2023. Delivery will be in the first quarter of 2022 and enable booster coverage throughout the year". As stated by the Minister for Health and Aged Care, Greg Hunt, "more than 280 million doses of COVID-19 vaccines have now been secured to support the COVID-19 roll-out". We are referring here to 280 million doses for a country with the population of only 26 million. And 8 billion of taxpayers' dollars have so far been invested in the Morrison government's COVID-19 vaccine rollout.[80] This is all happening although these COVID-19 vaccines are only 'provisionally' approved by the Therapeutic Goods Administration (TGA), which relies upon manufacturers' data and post-market assessment to judge the effectiveness and safety of these products.[81] 'Post market assessment' indicates people being part of the clinical trials assessing these products, as admitted by the Health Minister, when he candidly admits that "[t]he world is engaged in the largest clinical trial, the largest global vaccination trial ever."[82] The TGA website communicates two important things:

(a) Some countries are using versions of Emergency Use Authorisations (such as the UK, US and Canada) to urgently make vaccines available. This is because of the large number of COVID-19 cases and risk in those countries.

(b) The TGA has engaged early with pharmaceutical companies about their vaccines and is accepting rolling data. This means that the TGA can assess clinical trial date as it becomes available, rather than at the end of the clinical trial phases. This speeds up the review process.[83]

In other words, the government of many western nations, Australia included, are ostensibly by-passing years – up to ten years – of the usual long-term testing. Also, as noted by Dr Stephen Chavura, who is a historian and a political scientist, "some of these vaccinations are mRNA, which isn't a traditional form of vaccination". Therefore, the argument that these vaccines are fine in the long-term, because no past vaccine may have produced long-term adverse effects, is seriously misleading for two primary reasons:

(a) other vaccinations were long-term tested to address any such long-term effects before they made it to the general public;

(b) they didn't use mRNA technology, and we have no long-term data on the effect of mRNA vaccinations.

Would we be happy for future medicines to be produced as quickly as the COVID-19 vaccines? And if not, Dr Chavura asks rhetorically: "Does not that give us a reason to think that the production process of these vaccinations is a matter of concern, if not for the here and now then at least for the future given the precedent they set and the rule they may establish?"[84]

To make it worse, it is now patently clear that COVID-19 vaccines have prevented neither infection nor transmission. The purported 'protection' provided by these vaccines has shown to be of extremely limited duration, and now 'boosters' are being promoted, potentially for life. For example, the minimum gap for vaccine 'boosters' in the United Kingdom has been halved from six monthly to three monthly, which is due to the failure of these vaccines to provide an effective immunity to COVID-19.[85]

How many people knew they were being set up for a potential lifetime of boosters? With such low risks for most people, why are mass populations being coerced to be vaccinated with defective COVID-19 vaccines? Vaccination coercion adversely affects the civil rights of people and gives the government and employers an enormous amount of invasive power over their lives. If everyone eventually gets vaccinated due to coercive vaccination measures, then it proves vaccine mandates work and that people are basically happy to comply, which makes the government much easier to justify more coercive measures in the future. As a result, Dr Chavura concludes, mandatory vaccines would go from being only exceptions to the rule (the Nuremberg Code) to the new rule.

Sounds far-fetched? Remember when only two vaccinations were mandated? Now we are rolling into a third vaccine mandate, and they have barely started with the kids. Although COVID-19 does not pose any serious risk for them, children as young as five are being forced into vaccination even against the explicit will of their parents. Of course, the risk of children dying of COVID-19 is close to zero as this virus is far less dangerous to them than a normal influenza. Based on data coming from New York City (the hotbed of the pandemic in the United States), only 0.01 per cent of those under the age of 18 required hospitalisation from COVID-19.[86] One must consider that this is only about hospitalisation, and not death from the coronavirus. Of course, nothing is said here about all those who never became sick enough to even get tested for COVID-19, since about 86 per cent of infections are so mild that they are not even documented.

Dr John Ionnidis, professor of medicine and epidemiology at Stanford University, believes that the average rate of death for COVID-19, when adjusted from wide age range and unreported cases, could be as low as 0.05 per cent, similar to that of influenza.[87] He also explains that more than 80 per cent of those who get the virus have no symptoms or these symptoms are actually very mild. Of those under the 50s age group, at least 99.5 per cent will survive, which is less than the normal round of the flu.

In fact, even the World Health Organisation ('WHO') acknowledges that "[m]ost people infected with the virus will experience mild to moderate respiratory illness and recover without requiring especial treatment". With such low risks for most people, why is the entire population of Australia being coerced to be vaccinated with COVID-19 vaccines?

Indeed, Prime Minister Scott Morrison has announced that the COVID-19 vaccination program will be extended to all children aged 5 to 11 from 10 January 2022 after the Federal government accepted recommendations from the Australian Technical

Advisory Group ('ATAGI'). As stated on the website of the federal Department of Health, all children aged 5 to 11 "will receive 2 doses of the vaccine, 8 weeks apart. The children's dose one third of the dose for people aged 12 years and over".[88]

This is actually quite disgraceful because a study, conducted by King's College London scientists, has authoritatively concluded the overall risk of children becoming severely ill or dying of COVID-19 is "extremely low".[89] As a result, the U.K. government's Joint Committee on Vaccination and Immunisation (JCVI) has refused to endorse COVID-19 vaccination for children under the age of 18, stating that the benefit to them of receiving the novel vaccine is "virtually zero", whereas the already-known risk of serious harms are "not negligible".[90] On July 19, 2021, JCVI officially announced it was advising the U.K. government against the mass roll out of these novel vaccines to the healthy under the age of 18. "At this time", the statement concludes: "JCVI is of the view that the health benefits of universal vaccination in children and young people below the age of 18 years do not outweigh the potential risks".[91]

Just one known serious potential risk, or adverse effect of these novel vaccines, is that of myocarditis – inflammation of the heart. Myocarditis has a high rate of progressing to heart failure and is one of the reasons some younger people end up needing heart transplants. A recently published peer-reviewed paper produced by pharmacology/toxicology professors has examined these issues related to COVID-19 vaccinations for children. It concluded:

> The bulk of the official COVID-19 attributed death per capita oc-
> cur in the elderly with high comorbidities, and the COVID-19
> attributed deaths per capita are negligible in children ... Clinical
> trials for these inoculations were very short-term (a few months),
> had samples not representative of the total population, and for
> adolescents/children, had poor predictive power because of their
> small size. Further, the clinical trials did not address changes in
> biomarkers that could serve as early warning indicators of the el-

evated predisposition to serious diseases. Most importantly, the clinical trials did not address long-term effects that, if serious, would be borne by children/adolescents for potentially decades.

A novel best-case scenario cost-benefit analysis showed very conservatively that there are five times the number of deaths attributable to each inoculation vs those attributable to COVID-19 in the most vulnerable 65+ demographic. The risk of death from COVID-19 decreases drastically as age decreases, and the longer-term effects of the inoculations on lower age groups will increase their risk-benefit ratio, perhaps substantially. [92] (*emphasis added*)

So, given the already known potential harms of the novel vaccines, of which myocarditis is just one, and the entirely unknown potential long-term adverse effects which may come to light only after many years, the decision of the Morrison government to vaccinate everyone, including small children, regardless of age or health conditions, is plainly wrong and not scientific. This is clearly a political decision, not a medical one. Nor is it moral or ethical, because there are profoundly serious risks attached to any new drug and COVID-19 vaccines have limited short-term and no long-term safety date. As an article from the *British Medical Journal* explains:

> From a public health standpoint, it makes poor sense to impose vaccine side-effects on people at minimal risk of severe COVID-19. The argument that it protects others is weak or contrary to evidence. This conclusion suggests a policy of targeting vaccination to those at highest risk, allowing broader post-infection immunity to provide community protection.[93]

Richard Muller is an Emeritus Professor of Physics at the University of California-Berkeley. He is now entirely convinced that COVID-19 is "a million-to-one proposition to have arisen naturally". According to him, it is "extremely likely" the new coronavirus was deliberately created in that notorious lab at the Wuhan Institute of Virology in China, which curiously received millions of dollars from the National Institute of Allergy and

Infectious Diseases, headed by Anthony Fauci, the Chief Medical Advisor to the U.S. President.

Of course, one can only hope this persuasive theory that Covid-19 has 'escaped' from that CCP virus lab is just a coincidence. Regardless, the fact is that the response to the spread of the novel coronavirus certainly struck a very heavy blow at democracy by undermining the 'rule of law' and confidence that people have in the ruling classes, particularly in members of the legal, medical, and political professions. It has also fatally compromised the rights and freedoms of people and wrecking the economies of the free world. In such an environment, it is no wonder that people have come to distrust the proposed remedy to the problem of COVID-19 infection.

5

THE EXTERNAL AFFAIRS POWER AND VACCINE MANDATES

The political class in the Australian States is forcing the population to get vaccinated or face job losses and/or heavy fines. Some States and Territories have also issued so-called 'public health orders' which are vaccine mandates for certain industries and workers. Some Premiers have even decided that unvaccinated people will be treated as second-class citizens. For example, the website of the Queensland Government reveals that as from 17 December 2021 unvaccinated people are unable to:

- visit vulnerable settings, including hospitals, residential aged care, disability accommodation services, and prisons.

- attend hospitality venues such as hotels, pubs, clubs, taverns, bars, restaurants or cafes

- attend indoor entertainment venues such as nightclubs, live music venues, karaoke bars, concerts, theatres or cinemas

- attend outdoor entertainment activities such as sporting stadiums, theme parks or tourism experience like reef excursions

- attend festivals – either indoor or outdoor – such as musical festivals, folk festivals or arts festivals

- attend Queensland Government owned galleries, museums or libraries.[94]

In the name of "health", politicians can now happily implement the most unthinkable and atrocious perversities, especially vaccine mandates. In Victoria, the Parliament adopted the law that will give the Premier enhanced authoritarian powers, transferring the authority of the Chief Health Officer to the Premier, to declare a pandemic.

Amid such human-rights violations, there is the tacit support of the Prime Minister. The federal government's policy allegedly is that vaccinations are voluntary for most Australians, although its aim is to have as many people as possible to be vaccinated.

Scott Morrison has been critical of the mandatory vaccination laws imposed by State governments but will not back legislation that would effectively overturn their ability to impose them. A One Nation bill would have prohibited States, Territories and businesses from discriminating on the basis of whether a person was vaccinated. But it would also have prohibited the federal government from striking a funding agreement for public services with a State that imposed mandatory vaccinations.

Not only has the Prime Minister been tacitly supporting these arbitrary measures, but also objectively misleading the population by claiming that the Federal Government has no authority to 'override' any State laws and Executive orders that mandate vaccines and violate fundamental legal rights.

The rise and growth of international law has increased the size and significance of Australia's external affairs. The principle that the external affairs power now extends to allow the federal government to regulate any matters related to the protection of fundamental rights is commonly accepted by the courts.

The Australian Constitution, in its Section 51 (xxix), says:

> The Parliament shall, subject to this Constitution, have power to make laws for the peace, order, and good government of the Commonwealth with respect to … (xxix) External affairs.

The phrase 'external affairs' refers to persons, places, matters, or things geographically external to Australia. It enables the federal Parliament to pass any law concerning topics related to the protection of human rights, including the prohibition of compulsory vaccination.

The federal Executive can enter into international agreements as part of its general executive power under section 61. To become part of domestic law, treaties must be enacted by Parliament under section 51 (xxix).

The rise and growth of international law has dramatically increased the significance of the external affairs power. As the range of topics regulated under section 51(xxix) has been gradually expanded, federal legislation has more often come into conflict with State legislation. Accordingly, a federal law will be valid even on the ground of formal dealings of the federal Executive, which then could enable the Federal Parliament to legislate on fundamental rights and protections for the Australian citizen.[95]

As the range of topics that can be regulated under section 51(xxix) has expanded, the federal government has come into conflict with the States, which have at times expressed a discontentment with the supremacy of the Commonwealth legislative powers at the expense of their own powers. According to Bed Harris,

> Although the Commonwealth is able to incorporate international law such as treaties into domestic law by using s 51(xxix), should it find it expedient to do so, it is important to note that there is no rule of law obliging the Commonwealth to adhere to rules of international law when it exercises its legislative powers. In other words, if the Commonwealth chooses to disregard, or even leg-

islate in contravention of, rules of international law, there is no restraint on its doing so. The cynic may, therefore, say that the principles of international law can only be of benefit to the Commonwealth – they can be used as a platform for domestic legislation, but no domestic legislation will be invalid for inconsistency with international law. [96]

Sir Harry Gibbs, a former Australian Chief Justice, in a highly regarded academic article, explains that together with the regular operation of section 109 (inconsistency) of the Constitution, the external affairs power has the potential to 'annihilate State legislative power in virtually every respect'.[97] Gibbs concluded:

> It appears no exaggeration to say that the combined effect of s 51(xxix) and s 109 is that the Commonwealth can annihilate State legislative power in virtually every respect.[98]

Section 109 of the Constitution provides that federal laws must prevail over those of a State to the extent of any inconsistency. The State law is then deemed invalid to the extent of the inconsistency. Situations of conflict between a State law and a federal law arise, for example, when:

> a) the State law cannot be obeyed at the same time as the federal law (*Mabo v Queensland* (1988) 166 CLR 186);
>
> b) when the federal law permits a certain activity prohibited by a State law (*Colvin v Bradley Bros Pty Ltd* (1943) 68 CLR 151);
>
> c) when a federal law confers a right which a State law seeks to remove (*Clyde Engineering Co Ltd v Cowburn* (1926) 37 CLR 466).

The Australian government has entered into numerous treaties on a wide range of matters. In *R v Burgess; Ex parte Henry*, decided in 1936, the Court ruled that the external affairs power is not restricted to the Commonwealth's power to make laws with respect to the external aspects of the subjects mentioned in section 51.

This approach, according to Stewart and Williams, has allowed

> the specific Commonwealth powers to be applied in areas never contemplated by the framers. Seemingly innocuous powers like that over 'external affairs' have become major weapons in the Commonwealth armoury. Since the Tasmanian Dam case (1983) the High Court has accepted that this power can be used to pass laws that implement obligations that have been assumed by the federal government under international instruments like treaties and conventions ... Given that Australia, as at December 2005, had entered into 2544 international instruments, the possible uses of the external affairs power remain enormous. The fact that it can be used to legislate in areas formerly under State control is, according to the long accepted approach of the High Court, irrelevant.[99]

For a Commonwealth law to be constitutionally valid, a constitutional head of power must support it. The Commonwealth government has relied upon the external affairs power to support the enactment of numerous federal laws over the years. In particular, the Commonwealth government could enact a law, which prohibits mandatory vaccines at any level of government pursuant to Australia's entry into several international human rights instruments, thereby giving effect to these instruments.[100]

This reliance on international instruments should be evident from the Preamble to the proposed legislation.

Further, implementing these international human-rights instruments through the external affairs power would provide the basis on which the Commonwealth government could defend the constitutional validity of its legislation if this was challenged in the High Court. In this case, the Court would be able to decide that the federal law is valid law because the external affairs power supports its constitutionality.

As such, the question of whether the external affairs power supports the enactment of a federal law prohibiting compulsory vaccination by the Australian States is one that must be carefully considered. In fact, concerns were raised about the constitutionality of an anti-vaccine mandate bill, supported by One Nation, when it was introduced into the Australian Senate towards the end of November 2021. For example, Senator Eric Abetz, who failed to support the bill, argued that the federal Parliament did not have the legislative power to adopt the proposed law.

Ratifying an international treaty allows the Commonwealth government to legislate domestically to incorporate One Nation's proposed pro-choice law under the external affairs power. Of course, the legislation would have to meet the specificity and conformity requirements. But Australia entering a treaty is all that is necessary to meet this requirement.

In the *Tasmanian Dam Case*[101] and subsequent cases, the High Court has stated that "[t]he existence of international character or international concern is established by entry by Australia into the Convention or treaty".[102] Hence, the very fact that Australia has ratified a treaty or international legal agreement will be sufficient to satisfy any requirement of 'international character'. Furthermore, in *Pape v Federal Commissioner of Taxation*, Heydon J observed that "[t]he treaty or commitment need not have the precision necessary to establish a legally enforceable agreement at common law, but it must avoid excessive generality".[103]

In the Preamble of the World Health Organisation's Constitution, the word "health" is conceptualised as a "state of complete physical, mental and social well-being and not merely the absence of disease or infirmity". However, to allegedly defeat an apparently deadly virus, draconian measures have caused millions of people to endure highly stressful and traumatic situations, including home confinement, job losses, financial ruin, and a whole host of mental illnesses and challenges. These measures are unlawful not only in accordance with our system of democratic parliamentary government but also under international law. They unlawfully

A 'RULE OF LAW' PERSPECTIVE

affect the enjoyment of our fundamental rights and freedoms, including freedom of speech, association, movement, expression, and privacy.

"Seriously, one more comment about human rights ... it's about human life", complained Daniel Andrews, the Victorian Premier, about journalists who dare to question the impact on human rights of lockdown measures.[104] For Mr Andrews, "health" not only trumps human rights but shows that the right thing is doing what might be advantageous to the preservation of public health.

International law recognises that, during extraordinary circumstances, the States may enact emergency powers that suspend ordinary rule-of-law protections, with the exception however of "non-derogable rights". The inalienability of certain rights has been acknowledged by the *Siracusa Principles on the Limitation and Derogation Provisions in the International Covenant on Civil and Political Rights* ('Siracusa Principles'). A document produced by the American Association for the International Commission of Jurists, the Siracusa Principles, declares that:

> No state party shall, even in time of emergency threatening the life of the nation, derogate from the Covenant's guarantees of the right to life; freedom from torture, cruel, inhuman or degrading treatment or punishment, and from medical or scientific experimentation without free consent; freedom from slavery or involuntary servitude ... the right to recognition as a person before the law; and freedom of thought, conscience and religion. These rights are not derogable under any conditions even for the asserted purpose of preserving the life of the nation.[105]

As mentioned before, Australian governments are now starting to impose vaccination mandates as a way out of lockdowns. These governments communicate that the unvaccinated will be treated differently to the vaccinated, some even losing their jobs if they do not comply with the vaccination requirement. In practice, this means that unvaccinated individuals will have less freedoms to get a job, to travel and to socialise, and to go to coffee shops and restaurants.

This governmental approach creates a two-tier society that is unsupported by the *Nuremberg Code* – an ethics code – relied upon during the Nazi doctors' trials in Nuremberg in 1947. This Code has as its first principle the willingness and informed consent by the individual to receive medical treatment or to participate in an experiment.

Informed consent can be described as the voluntary agreement by an individual to a proposed medical or pharmaceutical treatment, given after sufficient and appropriate information about potential risks and benefits, i ncluding p ossible a dverse e ffects, how common they are, and what they should do about them.

From the perspective of international law, the right to informed consent is the bedrock principle of ethical standards in medicine. According to Article 6(1) of UNESCO's *Universal Declaration on Bioethics and Human Rights* (2005):

> Any preventive, diagnostic and therapeutic medical intervention is only to be carried out with the prior, free and informed consent of the person concerned, based on adequate information. The consent should, where appropriate, be express and may be withdrawn by the person concerned at any time and for any reason without disadvantage or prejudice.

As can be seen, international instruments prohibit the removal of non-derogable rights even in situations of an alleged "emergency", including the right to informed consent when it comes to vaccination. This prohibition encompasses any form of compulsion subjecting individuals to mandatory medical or pharmaceutical service, including vaccination.

In this context, Rocco Loiacono comments:

> For any government either by itself or via corporate proxy to attempt to mandate vaccines in circumstances were there has not been adequate testing and analysis of risks as well as benefits would constitute not only a violation of the principle of informed consent ... but a violation of Australia's obligations under international law with respect to medical experimentation.[106]

While the *International Covenant on Economic, Social and Cultural Rights ('ICESCR),* contains no definition of health, the United Nations' *Committee on Economic Social and Cultural Rights* communicates that the right to health contains both fundamental freedoms and entitlements. These freedoms include 'the right to control one's health and body', and 'the right to be free from non-consensual medical treatment and experimentation'.[107]

Under article 2(1) of ICESCR, Australia is legally obliged to take steps 'to the maximum of its available resources, with a view to achieving progressively the full realisation' of the fundamental rights recognised in the Convention. Article 2(1) of the ICESCR states:

> 1. Each State Party to the present Covenant undertakes to take steps, individually and through international assistance and co-operation, especially economic and technical, to the maximum of its available resources, with a view to achieving progressively the full realization of the rights recognized in the present Covenant by all appropriate means, including particularly the adoption of legislative measures.

The United Nations' *Committee on Economic Social and Cultural Rights* has determined that Article 2(1) "must be read in the light of the overall objective of the Covenant which is to establish clear obligations for States parties in respect of the full realization of the rights in question".

This provision, "thus imposes an obligation to move as expeditiously and effectively as possible towards that goal". Furthermore, in its Article 4, the ICESCR declares:

> The States Parties to the present Covenant recognize that, in the enjoyment of those rights provided by the State in conformity with the present Covenant, the State may subject such rights only to such limitations as are determined by law only in so far as this may be compatible with the nature of these rights and solely for the purpose of promoting the general welfare in a democratic society. [108]

The United Nations' *Committee on Economic Social and Cultural Rights* emphasises that the Covenant's limitation clause to be found in Article 4, "is primarily intended to protect the rights of individuals rather than to permit the imposition of limitations by States". As also noted by the Committee, "issues of public health are sometimes used by States as grounds for limiting the exercise of other fundamental rights".[109]

Consequently, any State, which, for example, restricts the movement of, or incarcerates, persons with transmissible diseases, refuses to allow doctors to treat persons believed to be opposed to a government, is acting in a manner that is "incompatible with the nature of the rights protected by the ICESCR".[110]

In addition, Article 12.2. of the ICESCR acknowledges that the right to health embraces a wide range of fundamental rights which allows people to have a healthy life, such as employment rights and freedoms to movement and association.

Yet, these fundamental freedoms are being profoundly undermined in Australia. The Australian government is directly in conflict with these freedoms.

In George Orwell's dystopian novel, 1984, the *New Thought Police* were able to control the ideas that determined the political and cultural values of society. The withdrawal of personal freedoms was sold in Australia as a positive thing. Slavery to the State was presented as the gateway to freedom and prosperity.

Some crimes are committed by commission and others by

omission. The Morrison government is surely guilty of the latter. It had the authority to override State laws which violate fundamental rights and freedoms.[111] However, the Prime Minister says there is nothing his government can do. This view is certainly erroneous, and one does not need to be a prophet to predict that dark days will descend upon Australia.

In a recent interview on Perth Radio 6PR about her view on vaccine mandates, Australian Human Rights Commissioner, Lorraine Finlay, warned that governments need to be careful, from a human-rights perspective, about imposing broad vaccine mandates across the country. While governments can limit some rights to protect public health, these measures, according to her, "always need to be justified, non-discriminatory and proportionate".[112] She further explained that, while targeted vaccine mandates have existed before COVID-19, to impose such mandates on the entire population is to navigate in rather "unchartered territory". As Finlay correctly points out, "what's really important is to make sure that mandates are targeted to risk rather than simply imposed in a blanket way".[113]

Former Liberal MP Craig Kelly was viciously criticised by the Prime Minister and other members of the federal Parliament for his apparent endorsement of drugs that have provided an effective treatment against COVID-19. Kelly had published on his Facebook page a number of peer-reviewed papers written by leading medical academics and experts supporting such alternative treatments. His comment on Ivermectin, for example, was based on the research of immunologist Robert Clancy from Newcastle University. In an interview with 6PR in January 2021, Professor Clancy commented that the use of hydroxychloroquine and Ivermectin was "clearly effective" in the fight against the COVID-19 virus. As an expert in the field, he was explaining the facts and results as he carefully interpreted them.

The evidence for Ivermectin is based on a series of academic research, suggesting the treatment is entirely effective against the coronavirus. One of these studies on the drug's efficacy and safety was led by Dr Ahmed Elgazzar from Benha University. Published on the Research Square website in December 2020, it provides reliable evidence on the effectiveness of early interventions due to the minimum risk of confounding factors influencing the results. In summary, the empirical study found that patients with COVID-19 treated in hospital who received Ivermectin early reported substantial recovery, and there was "a substantial improvement and reduction in mortality rate in ivermectin treated groups by 90 per cent".[114]

The World Health Organisation and the National Institute of Health (U.S.) have both endorsed the treatment, with India successfully treating the population with hydroxychloroquine and Ivermectin plus zinc supplements. The combined use of the two drugs have been successfully used to treat the COVID-19 disease in India, the Czech Republic, and some States in the United States. By contrast, countries such as Israel that have their population almost entirely vaccinated are experiencing a dramatic increase in coronavirus infections.

Israel has been held up as the "gold standard" of how to carry out coronavirus vaccine rollouts. However, in August 2021, the country's Prime Minister Naftali Bennett openly confessed that the Pfizer vaccine "is significantly less" effective against the Delta variant. In a 5th August 2021 interview with an Israeli television station (Channel 13), Dr Kobi Haviv, who is medical director of Herzog Hospital in Jerusalem, stated that most of its coronavirus patients are vaccinated, including those with severe disease. Dr Haviv further specified that 95 per cent of the severe patients were fully vaccinated, adding that "85.90% of the hospitalizations are in fully vaccinated people", thus forcing that hospital to open "more and more COVID wards". This has led him to conclude that the effectiveness of the Pfizer-BioNTech vaccine at preventing coronavirus infections is now reduced to only 39 per cent, and it is effectively "fading out".[115]

This might be too much for our political class to handle. Rather than defending the right of people to have their opinions and seek alternative medical treatments, the Prime Minister reprimands politicians for supporting these treatments. "The views expressed by the member for Hughes do not align with my views, or the views of the advice that has been provided to me by the Chief Medical Office", Scott Morrison told Parliament in February 2021. The Prime Minister wants 95 per cent of the population taking the vaccine, although people under 60 have a small chance of dying of the virus. He wants to make vaccination as mandatory as possible.[116] "I expect that it would be as mandatory as you can possibly make it", Mr Morrison stated in August 2020.[117] His comments followed the signing of Australia's first vaccine deal with drug maker AstraZeneca.[118]

As mentioned above, a full fact-check testifies that some alternative treatments have been successfully used to treat the COVID-19 disease in India, the Czech Republic and some States in the United States. The Prime Minister should allow people the right to seek these alternative treatments. Ironically, the federal government that bans therapeutics like hydroxychloroquine and zinc, is the same government that miserably failed to protect nursing homes where the highest incidence of Covid victims has occurred. The false mantra that governments must follow their cherry-picked 'health experts' to impose dramatic restrictions on the basic freedoms of the citizen must be urgently challenged.

6

PATERNALISM AND VACCINE MANDATES

The main argument of this book is that vaccine mandates facilitate the creation of a fundamentally unfair and unequal society where vaccinated people are privileged and the unvaccinated become second-class citizens who are excluded from most activities of normal life and are regarded as lepers in their own country.

In his Australia Day 2021 message, Prime Minister Scott Morrison proclaimed that "We are a decent, fair, enterprising, and generous people who respond to whatever challenge is put before us. We are a people 'one and free' who look out for each other and our neighbours and are always striving to do better." This is undoubtedly an inspirational message which, however, has been revealed to be untrue in Australia in 2021. On December 17 2021, as Australia was just a week away from Christmas, the decency and the fairness the prime minister spoke about was suppressed, illegally and immorally, by the State government of Queensland.

As from that day, the unvaccinated in Queensland are no longer allowed to visit clubs, restaurants, cafés, theatres, museums, and libraries. Even supermarkets will have the option to exclude unvaccinated customers.[119] These capricious orders have turned

Queensland into a deeply segregationist state where some people are treated with blatant discrimination. Such draconian and totalitarian measures had never been adopted in Australia before. Indeed, that day has gone down in history as a day of infamy for four reasons.

First, these arbitrary rules involve the entrenchment of institutional discrimination against a minority of law-abiding citizens. They involve the distribution of burdens and benefits on the ground of vaccine status. They introduce a system of apartheid, a two-tier Australia.

Second, the obtuse rules mandating the discriminatory treatment of citizens based on their vaccine status are illegal because they effectively abrogate the right of individuals to consent to medical treatment, including vaccinations. As mentioned, the Nuremberg Code, relied upon during the Nazi doctors' trials in 1947, supports the right of an individual to refuse vaccinations. This ethics code has as its first principle the willingness and informed consent by the individual to receive medical treatment or to participate in a medical experiment.

Third, the discriminatory Queensland rules add to the cost of doing business. This is because the establishments, which the unvaccinated may not visit, must ensure that only vaccinated people be admitted to their premises. Hence, the rules really impose an obligation on these businesses to function as police officers to enforce the orders, thereby becoming accessories to a profoundly immoral activity. These businesses are subject to heavy fines if they admit unvaccinated visitors to their premises. A zealous, and politicised police force, is aware that a few businesses are reluctant to enforce the discriminatory rule; consequently, the police will undoubtedly target these businesses.

Fourth, the rules are complex and forever changing. It becomes necessary to constantly check the Queensland Health website to ascertain whether it is possible to travel to this or that region of the State and, if so, what documents must be carried, or obtained to travel. The transitory nature of these health orders adversely affects the realisation of the rule of law, which invariably requires stability. However, endless changes in government health orders or commands make it extremely hard, if not impossible, for anyone to plan their lives according to predictable legal standards.

The impact of COVID-19 health orders on the lives of people is truly staggering. The interminable lockdown and border closures have wrought havoc and inflicted misery on many people. Each day, people are inundated with fluid and ever-changing directions which, however, are hardly transparent.

This idea of constant change was captured perceptively by Michael Dimarco in an article in *The Spectator* when the stated that, "One of the great ironies of the COVID-19 pandemic is how **consistent** Western governments have been at providing **inconsistent** health advice." (emphasis added).[120] The ever-changing nature and lack of transparency of the COVID-19 orders have made it difficult for people to plan their lives. It may also have adversely affected the nature of Australia's liberal democratic system.

These constant episodes of heinous institutionalised discrimination, fuelled by numerous and predictably unpredictable health orders, reveal that Australian governments have learnt little from history. It is a fair guess that most Australian politicians have never heard of the Roman historian Tacitus, who noted that, "The more corrupt the state, the more numerous the laws." This is not likely to change soon, considering that the mandarins of the school curriculum have seen to it that the teaching of history is neglected, thereby ensuring that Australians remain ignorant of their own and international history.

The inflexible implementation of controversial vaccine mandates has resulted in the abrogation of society's expectation of equal treatment of citizens. These mandates are unconstitutional and illegal and violate Australia's understanding of the 'rule of law'. They also potentially lead to 'mass formation', which according to Dr Mattias Desmet can be "the first step toward totalitarianism and atrocity in the name of collective welfare."

Vaccine mandates, imposed by Australian governments are examples of paternalism that compromise and erode Australian values and traditions. The collapse of Australian values and traditions, especially the abandonment of 'equality' as an overriding Australian characteristic, is an unfortunate 'side-effect' of mandatory vaccination. These values and traditions have irretrievably been compromised by governments' insistence that everyone should be vaccinated with a COVID-19 vaccine.

In this Chapter, we discuss the paternalism that underlies the imposition of vaccine mandates by State governments. By way of example, we also consider the emerging phenomenon of 'dobbing-in', which appears to be an ill-fated 'side-effect' of vaccine mandates, and indeed of most COVID-19 orders, which has changed the Australia most people would have known, or at least recognised, until a few years ago.

In an interesting article published in *The Atlantic*, Conor Friedersdorf admits that "Australia is undoubtedly a democracy, with multiple political parties, regular elections, and the peaceful transfer of power." However, he then rhetorically asks the question whether Australia is still a liberal democracy:

> But if a country indefinitely forbids its own citizens from leaving its borders, strands tens of thousands of its citizens abroad, puts strict rules on intrastate travel, prohibits citizens from leaving home without an excuse from an official government list, mandates masks even when people are outdoors and socially distanced, deploys the military to enforce those rules, bans protest,

and arrests and fines dissenters, is that country still a liberal democracy?[121]

Friedersdorf's question implies that the unrelenting and inflexible
use of power under the relevant Public Health Acts have
transformed Australia into an illiberal police State characterised
by bureaucratic zeal and lack of transparency.

For sure, one can only be amazed by the unpredictability and
absurdity of some Directions imposed by Australia's health
bureaucracies on people. Two examples will suffice to illustrate
this point.

Prior to the re-opening of the border on 13 December 2021, if
residents from New South Wales wanted to relocate to Queensland,
they had to fulfil all requirements stated in their Queensland
Border Declaration, including evidence of their residency in
the approved form. They were then provided with an allocated
entry date and designated entry airport to enter Queensland
which had been confirmed by a government authority when they
received their pass.[122] Typically, a person proposing to relocate
to Queensland was expected to wait for ten business days before
receiving an answer from the relevant health quango. However,
the Queensland authorities since announced that this period could
highly likely be extended because there were many applications
for relocation to Queensland. This extended period was needed to
ensure that there were sufficient quarantine hotel rooms available
to accommodate the new arrivals.

In this context, the Health Administration's inability to
communicate to applicants revealed a lack of transparency
because it failed to indicate when applicants would be provided
with an answer. The Administrations also failed to communicate
how many quarantine rooms were available at any time. Yet, this
information was essential to facilitate the relocation plans of
applicants, quite apart from, and in addition to, the expectation

that the Administration would fully inform the public of its COVID-19 response.

The second example concerned the deliveries of alcohol to residents of apartment blocks locked down by New South Wales Health. These deliveries were policed to limit the daily consumption of drinks. Specifically, residents were only entitled to one six-pack of beer, or one wine bottle, or a 375 ml of spirits a day. This rule was introduced to ensure the safety of their staff and residents.[123] It would be interesting to ascertain whether the police service ever contemplated checking the shopping orders of people to ensure this edict was not violated.

Such examples of administrative overkill have fuelled the media's doomsday predictions that point to the development of a two-tier Australian society. The former Premier of New South Wales has warned that, "Unvaccinated people in New South Wales could be barred from locations and denied movement freedoms even after the state achieves 80% double dose vaccination" and that, "vaccine-hesitant residents … will not be able to "let everybody else do the hard work and then turn up" for equal freedoms."[124] In the same vein, the former Deputy Premier of New South Wales boldly declared that businesses that accept unvaccinated people will be subject to exceptionally heavy fines. Private employers are encouraged to require their workforce to be vaccinated. These are draconian edicts, which will result in a two-tier Australia where some people will be deemed to be superior to others, involving the distribution of burdens and benefits simply on the ground of peoples' vaccine status.

The intrusive intervention of the health bureaucracies into the lives of law-abiding citizens reveals that governments have shamelessly embraced paternalism as a principle of legislation. The implementation of this principle results in the imposition of unpopular and burdensome health decisions which individuals should make themselves. These health bureaucracies and politicians are, in effect, embracing the 'Nanny State' which seeks to achieve its objectives, by prescriptively controlling, forbidding, or compelling the behaviour of individuals. In the context of COVID-19, the 'Nanny State' coerces its citizens, sometimes against their will, to vaccinate, or to be relegated to the status of a second-class citizen.

The term 'Nanny State' describes the tendency of many governments in this COVID-19 era to treat their "citizens as children in a nursery",[125] supervising and influencing their choices according to the health authorities' view of their well-being. Such an approach is "authoritarian and paternalistic … imposing on people what is good for them, for 'nanny knows best'."[126]

Underlying this philosophy is the notion that the State can make better choices for citizens than those citizens would make for themselves if left to their own devices. This worldview seeks to protect people even where they do not want protection, "over-riding consumer preferences to improve public health."[127] The daunting prospect of a two-tier Australian society is that, even when the COVID-19 pandemic has receded, Australia will have irretrievably changed for the worse. This is because peoples' rights will likely depend on the largesse of a supposedly mag-nanimous government that could easily take them away at the slightest provocation, especially in the field of health.

An interesting 'side effect' of the COVID-19 pandemic and the imposition of vaccine mandates, lost in the avalanche of information and disinformation that has characterised the vaccine debate, is that, increasingly, more Australians are tipping off police about alleged breaches of health orders, thereby policing the two-tier development of Australia. This issue is exemplified by the dobbing in of a former Prime Minister, Tony Abbott, for failing to wear a face mask, for which he was fined $500. But the possibilities for dobbing-in unvaccinated Australians, especially if they visit an establishment they are excluded from, are almost limitless.

There is no doubt that the pandemic has accelerated the trend of dobbing-in (also known as snitching) for alleged violations of COVID-19 restrictions, lockdowns and border closures that happened with monotonous regularity before the re-opening of State borders, following the imposition of vaccine mandates. By any standard, the steady stream of complaints is itself becoming an epidemic.

One only needs to look at the spectacular increase in the number of complaints received by the authorities following recent protests against lockdowns in Sydney – New South Wales Police received over 20,000 tip-offs.

Of course, the dobbing-in phenomenon is not new.

On 9 December 2002, the *Sydney Morning Herald* published a provocative story entitled 'The new culture of dobbing'. It noted that Australia is "a dobber's paradise" and that during the tail end the 20th century, "it would have been unthinkable, positively unAustralian" to dob-in your neighbours, but that now "ordinary members of the public are bombarded with offers to turn informant against fellow citizens."[128] Since then, the many environmental management rules – driven partly by the global warming movement – has propelled people into dobbing-in those deemed to have violated these new standards and regulations.

In the process, it has become common for individuals to observe others more closely. Hence, when people are observed throwing waste on the footpath, littering the bush, wasting water, or dropping lighted cigarette butts, they would often be reported to the authorities. On 23 December 2009, a Tasmanian newspaper, *The Mercury*, published in Hobart, similarly claimed that Australia has now become "a nation of dobbers" and that Australians have become "world-class informers" who dob in tax dodgers as well as "welfare rorters, criminals, litterbugs and water wasters."

The trend has gained traction, with many institutions introducing hotlines for people to register complaints. For example, the New South Wales police website allows complaints to be made online. The Commonwealth Department of Health and many other organisations, such as Ad Standards, have dedicated websites for people to complain about their neighbours. In addition, many hotlines allow complaints to be made anonymously, with some sizable financial rewards if a conviction can be obtained against a presumed miscreant.

The development of a dobbing-in culture, especially in a society divided by vaccine mandates, is worrying for a variety of reasons. Hence, it is necessary to consider whether this culture is un-Australian. What is the effect of this development on Australia's 'mateship' philosophy?

Australia inherited the verb 'to dob' from the British. In Australia, however, the word was hardly ever used prior to the 1950s, possibly because it was deemed to be un-Australian to dob-in your neighbour – a tradition going back to convict times. Bruce Moore, in an informative article entitled *The story of 'dob'* explains that the verb "to dob" was used in English dialects in the 19th century, and it had several meanings, only one of which means "to incriminate" or "to inform upon". He notes:

> It has long been a taboo in Australian society to dob on people, especially on one's mates, but more generally on anybody. This probably has something to do with the fact that any such dobbing in is usually to an 'authority', and therefore runs counter to the strong streak of anti-authoritarianism in the Australian psyche. It also runs counter to the notion of mateship and the fair go.[129]

Moore's explanation of the British origins of 'to dob' may remind readers of Donald Horne's iconic book *The Lucky Country*, published in 1964. Horne controversially wrote that, "Australia is a lucky country run mainly by second rate people who share its luck."[130] In 1976, in his follow-up book *Death of the Lucky Country*, Horne explained that the phrase 'The Lucky Country' "came from the luck of its historical origins ... We simply went along with some British habits."[131]

One really wonders what the motivation is of people who facilitate the development of the new dobbing-in culture. Is it jealousy of success, or is it the tall poppy syndrome that abrogates the right of people to a benefit that other people cannot have? Or is there a heightened sense of civic responsibility that propels people to inform on others who allegedly try to navigate around the myriad of obscure and ever-changing COVID-19 orders?

The dobbing-in culture has become endemic, even to the extent that this kind of behaviour may well be regarded as un-Australian, clashing with Australia's mateship philosophy, and rugged individualism. Is the extra-ordinary high number of complaints symptomatic of a society at war with itself and, more generally, of a fundamental change in Australian culture? Regardless, Australia's COVID-19 legacy has defaced Australia for ever and turned it into a potentially illiberal State, maintained by paternalistic laws.

7

EMERGENCY POWERS AND CIVIL DISOBEDIENCE

It is important to consider that the requirements of democratic government are directly derived from our liberal-democratic traditions, which seeks to promote the protection of individual rights and freedoms. As stated by Justice Gaudron *in Australian Capital Television Pty Ltd v Commonwealth*,[132] "the notion of a free society governed in accordance with the principles of representative parliamentary democracy may entail freedom of movement, freedom of association and … freedom of speech generally".[133]

When a legitimate form of representative government is constitutionally established, such government "hath no other end but the preservation of these rights, and therefore can never have a right to destroy, enslave, or designedly to impoverish the subjects".[134] Accordingly, the establishment of democratic government is an artefact conceived for a purpose. The great philosopher John Locke (1634-1704) was noticeably clear: our most fundamental rights are independent of, and antecedent to, the formation of government. If we let ourselves to be excessively controlled by government, then we are sacrificing our own sense of dignity and basically become enslaved. As noted by Locke in his chapter entitled 'On Slavery':

> This freedom from absolute, arbitrary power, is so necessary to, and closely joined with a man's preservation, that he cannot part with it, but by what forfeits his preservation and life together: for a man, not having the power of his own life, cannot, by compact, or his own consent, enslave himself to any one, nor put himself under the absolute, arbitrary power of another.[135]

In this sense, the right to disobey government directives that violate these fundamental freedoms constitutes a long-standing tradition in western legal-political philosophy. For example, a sound doctrine of resistance to arbitrary government was developed in the 17th century by Samuel Rutherford (1600-1661). In *Lex Rex* he explained that a political power whenever used to oppress it is not a lawful power but, instead, "a licentious deviation of a lawful power".[136]

These views were also expressed by St Thomas Aquinas, whose analysis amounts to "a prescription for limited government, providing a rational basis on which to affirm that there are limits to what the state can rightly do. Aquinas's insistence that the power of the human law be limited implies a "right" of the person not to be subjected to an unjust law."[137] According to Aquinas, "man is bound to obey secular rulers in so far as this is required by the order of justice. Wherefore if the political ruler commands what is unjust, his subjects are not bound to obey him, except perhaps accidentally in order to avoid scandal or danger."[138] Ultimately, Aquinas stated:

> If it is a people's right to provide itself with a political ruler, and if that ruler tyrannically abuses the power, there is no injustice if the community deposes or checks him whom they have raised to the government nor can it be charged with a breach of faith for abandoning a tyrant, even if the people had previously bound themselves to him; because, by not faithfully conducting himself in government as the public office demands, he has brought it on himself if his subjects renounce their bargain with him.[139]

Locke, who played a fundamental role in the development of constitutionalism, established that no government has legitimacy to undermine inalienable rights to life, liberty, and property. As he put it:

> Whenever the legislators endeavour to take away and destroy the property of the people [i.e., their basic rights to life, liberty, and property], or to reduce them to slavery under arbitrary power, they put themselves into a state of war with the people, who are thereupon absolved from any further obedience, and are left to the common refuge which God hath provided for all men against force and violence.[140]

The American Founders relied on Locke's phraseology to draft their 1776 Declaration of Independence, which evokes a "long train of abuses" and the "consent of the governed" as the primary basis for resistance against arbitrary government. Drawing heavily from Locke's philosophy, the American Declaration assumes the pre-eminence of the "Law of Nature" which prohibits government to violate our inalienable rights. Curiously, that same Declaration concludes that "whenever any form of government becomes destructive of these ends, it is the right of the people to alter or to abolish it, and to institute new government".

The practice of civil disobedience can be described as the violation of unjust legislation promulgated by the recognised governmental authority. The *International Covenant on Civil and Political Rights* ('ICCPR') does not mention civil disobedience as a potential right to resist governmental oppression, although it could be reasonably stated that some acts of disobedience are effectively protected by Articles 18 and 19 of this international Covenant. Under its Article 19, "everyone shall have the right to freedom of expression". And as stated by Article 18 of the ICCPR, "everyone shall have the right to freedom of thought, conscience and religion".

It is possible, therefore, to sustain an argument that citizens are morally justified to disobey legislative commands that are incompatible with well-known principles of the rule of law which are also derived from our traditions of constitutional government. Assume, for example, that the people find themselves in the uncomfortable situation of having to break a law to preserve their fundamental legal rights. Accordingly, the need of government to respect our freedoms of association, movement, speech and thought implies a natural right to breach rules which are inconsistent with the ordinary exercise of these freedoms.

Since the primary purpose of representative democracy is the preservation of fundamental rights and freedoms, one must conclude that citizens have a lawful right to resist measures that grossly violate the enjoyment of these basic rights and freedoms. Accordingly, it is entirely reasonable to assume that any command by the State which directly violates these rights and freedoms is not law properly so called and certainly is not valid law from this constitutional perspective. In *Nationwide News Pty Ltd v Wills*[141], Justice Brennan said: "… where a representative democracy is constitutionally entrenched, it carries with it those legal incidents which are essential to the effective maintenance of government".[142] In other words, once it is judicially recognised that a representative democracy is constitutionally prescribed, then the preservation of fundamental rights and freedoms is "essential to sustain it as firmly entrenched in the Constitution as the system of government which the Constitution explicitly ordains".[143]

The emergence of a period of capricious authoritarianism in the history of Australia has revealed the ugliness, hidden until recently. Undoubtedly, Australia's health bureaucracies have adopted oppressive policies, arguably to safeguard the health of citizens.

However, the unrelenting, inflexible, and disproportionate use of unchecked power, characterised by the QR code tyranny, superimposed with very intrusive facial recognition technology, has made Australians into a compliant and docile population. Private employers, who encourage their workforce to vaccinate, support vaccine mandates, imposed by state health bureaucracies.

For example, Qantas has announced that all people who want to fly internationally, including its workforce, will need to be vaccinated. The Catholic Archbishop of Brisbane, Mark Coleridge, has issued a vaccine deadline for priests and deacons in his diocese. Even the local bridge clubs in Brisbane now require all players to be fully vaccinated by 17 December, when the Queensland state border is scheduled to be open, at least to fully vaccinated people.

These are draconian edicts, which will result in a two-tier Australia where some people are more privileged than others, involving the distribution of burdens and benefits simply on the ground of people's vaccine status. The predictable unpredictability, which is so typical of the imposition of health orders, is a response to the arrival in Australia of new variants of the COVID-19 virus, including the most recent, Omicron, which resulted in the closing of Australia's international borders.

As argued in Chapter Six, the intrusive intervention of the health bureaucracies and compliant businesses into the lives of law-abiding citizens reveals that governments have shamelessly embraced paternalism as a principle of legislation. The implementation of this principle results in the imposition of intrusive health decisions which individuals should be making themselves. These bureaucracies and politicians are, in effect, embracing the "Nanny State" which seeks to achieve its objectives, by prescriptively controlling, forbidding, or compelling the behaviour of individuals. Indeed, the "Nanny State" is coercive, for example, by compelling people to vaccinate or to stay at home and lose their rights.

So, the question "What could people do, if anything at all?" should be asked. This question requires us to delve deeper into the topic of civil disobedience.

Before addressing the mysteries of civil disobedience, it is useful to refer to a sobering statistic. In 2008, George Roberts, discussing an international survey on ABC News, reported that half of Australia's population cannot read or write properly. Since then, this percentage may have increased because "reading" and "writing" are flexible concepts. A deficient education system that despises Western civilisation and promotes political correctness has facilitated this rapid decline. This is a relevant statistic because a person's reading and writing abilities affect their capacity to think, and therefore they become obedient and slavish accepters of government propaganda, and proponents of the atrocious transformation of Australia into an illiberal state. Thus, civil disobedience requires people to be able to think for themselves.

In the context of COVID-19, civil disobedience may involve a deliberate violation of a mandatory vaccination mandate on the ground that the mandate is incompatible with "higher" moral or religious principles, civil rights, or natural rights. An assessment of the appropriateness of an act of civil disobedience depends, at least in part, on the extent to which the disobedient behaviour is "rational." The identification of its essential features could clarify the meaning of "rationality."

First, an act of civil disobedience could be judged by its effectiveness, namely its prospect of success. The effectiveness of an act affects its rationality because an ineffective act is not likely to have any societal impact and, hence, may not result in social change.

Second, a commitment to rationality requires that the higher principles, invoked by the lawbreaker as justification for an act of disobedience, are balanced against other "higher" principles that require obedience to orders imposed by government authorities.

Third, the rationality of an act of disobedience is judged by the willingness of a lawbreaker to accept the penalty imposed for breaching a vaccination order. This is because the willingness to accept the penalty proves that the lawbreaker adheres to the existing legal system while, at the same time, expressing his or her disagreement with the imposition of vaccine mandates. The willingness of the lawbreaker to accept punishments to eradicate the targeted injustices awakens the conscience of society.

Fourth, the requirement that an act of civil disobedience be rational also requires that the action be commensurate with the alleged injustice which caused a person to disobey the law. Thus, there is a requirement of proportionality. In this context, many health orders imposed on people are ridiculously disproportionate to the objectives the health bureaucracies and oppressive governments want to achieve.

These four requirements – effectiveness, striking a healthy balance, willingness to accept the penalty, and proportionality – guarantee that an act of civil disobedience is rational. These requirements ensure that an ardent desire to rectify egregious violations of civil rights motivates persons who contemplate civil disobedience.

Undoubtedly, there are several reasons why civil disobedience takes place. In general, civil disobedience becomes a societal problem when the normal channels of social change do not function properly anymore, or when the authorities disregard serious grievances.

A system does not function anymore when privileged groups have entrenched power positions in society and use their power to impose their will on weaker or vulnerable classes of people. This is precisely what may be happening in our COVID-19 era.

Civil disobedience, with an intent to challenge disproportionate health orders, is an example of legitimate political activity. So, it is a most appropriate and acceptable way to respond to the oppression by the health oligarchy and governments bent on increasing their power.

Professor Friedrich Hayek, the well-known Austrian economist, reminded us that "even a strong tradition of political liberty is no safeguard if the danger is precisely that new institutions and policies will gradually undermine and destroy that spirit" of liberty. For him, people are only able to save themselves if the spirit of liberty "reasserts itself in time and the people not only throw out the party which has been leading them further and further in the dangerous direction but also recognize the nature of the danger and resolutely change their course." Of course, we entirely agree with him.

In the context of COVID-19 protests, the question should be asked whether demonstrations against restrictions, mandatory vaccination, lockdowns, and border restrictions that have occurred in most capital cities of Australia can be characterised as 'civil disobedience'. In Melbourne, demonstrations turned violent when construction workers marched against the prolonged lockdown. Thousands of protesters assembled on Saturday, 6 November 2021, to protest the vaccine mandates of the Victorian government and its controversial *Public Health and Wellbeing Amendment (Pandemic Management) Bill* 2021 which gives the Premier unprecedented power to rule by decree.[144]

In a thoughtful article, *Civil Disobedience in Times of Pandemic: Clarifying Rights and Duties*, Yoann Della Croce and Ophelia Nicole-Berva argue that demonstrations do not qualify as 'civil disobedience' because the present COVID-19 restrictions are "limited in time" and people will eventually recover their civil rights.[145] These authors may well be right, but not for the reasons given in their article. This is because the protests have failed to change the State's management of the COVID-19 pandemic and, as such, they are demonstrably ineffective; they do not satisfy the first essential feature discussed above. It could be argued that ineffective protests do not qualify as 'civil disobedience.'

'Civil disobedience' is a deliberate breach of a valid law, regulation, or order on the ground that it violates a 'higher' principle, for example, a moral or religious principle. Even disregarding the claim that COVID-19 health orders lack parliamentary oversight and involve rulemaking by the Executive, they are validly enacted orders. However, in the context of the pandemic, protesters may claim that these orders abrogate higher principles, including human and civil rights, which exist independently of the legal system and are non-derogable. In contrast, the authors of the article, in arguing that, over time, people will recover these rights, imply that the State confers these rights on people and that the State can also suspend or repeal these rights to protect public health. On this line of argument, these rights do not exist prior to the establishment of civil society, and they do not constitute 'natural' rights.

Professor Carl Cohen makes a distinction between direct and indirect forms of civil disobedience.[146] In a COVID-19 context, direct disobedience involves a breach of the valid health order which protestors deem to be incompatible with "higher principles." Indirect disobedience involves the violation of a law or regulation that is not (or is only indirectly or remotely) related to the object of the protest. The Melbourne COVID-19 protests fall into either category because a vaccination refusal involves a direct violation of the vaccination mandate, whereas the desecration of the Shrine of Remembrance may be an example of an indirect form of disobedience.

It is problematic to characterise the Melbourne (and similar) protests as examples of 'civil disobedience.' This is because these protests are ineffective and their impact on society is negligible, and they do not result in desired change. Behaviour that directly targets the object of protest – for example, a vaccination mandate – is likely to be more effective than that which is only indirectly, or even remotely, connected to the impugned health order.

The demonstrators' willingness to accept the penalty imposed for breaching a valid health order may also affect the effectiveness of a protest. In accepting the penalties for their behaviour, demonstrators show their support for the State's existing legal system, and, at the same time, they express their disagreement with the management of the COVID-19 pandemic.

The effectiveness of protests, and their concomitant characterisation as 'civil disobedience,' also depends on the extent to which they are proportionate to the achievement of the demonstrators' objective of changing the State's COVID-19 narrative.

The violence surrounding the Melbourne protests raises the question whether the behaviour of demonstrators should be non-violent to qualify as an act of 'civil disobedience.' Although in most cases, protests should be non-violent in nature, there may well be instances of societal injustice which only violent protests could remedy.

To evaluate the effectiveness of a demonstration, it may also be necessary to consider the ability of demonstrators to analyse the nature and consequences of the State's COVID-19 strategy. If George Roberts's comment according to which half of Australia's population cannot read or write properly is valid, then there are likely to be problems in this area.[147] This is relevant because people who cannot read and write properly, may find it difficult to evaluate the purpose and consequences of their behaviour and, hence, may either obediently and slavishly accept the State's health orders, or participate in rebellious activity that has no prospect of success. This situation may be exacerbated when, according to Adam Carey, writing in *The Age*, four out of five teachers considered leaving the teaching profession during the COVID-19 pandemic.[148]

Nevertheless, the germs of rebellious behaviour are sown when the normal channels of social change do not function properly, or when serious grievances are not heard. A system does not function optimally when preferred groups have entrenched power positions in society and use their power to impose their will on weaker or vulnerable classes of people. The COVID-19 pandemic has contributed to the development of a two-tier Australian society where a powerful health bureaucracy has been able to impose its will on weaker, and less powerful, sections of the society.

Even when the COVID-19 pandemic is over – and this may take a long time – Australia will have changed irretrievably. This is because the civil rights of Australians will from now on always depend on the largesse of a magnanimous government bureaucracy that could easily take them away at the slightest provocation, especially in the field of health. Hence, a confident assertion that health orders are only time-constrained nuisances, and that people will recover their civil rights may be an optimistic expectation or an injudicious interpretation of the nature of the COVID-19 health orders.

8

LESSONS FROM THE TOTALITARIAN PAST

As mentioned in Chapter Two, contemporary definitions of the concept of legality known as the rule of law often start with the views expressed by Albert Venn Dicey (1835–1922). This 19th-century English constitutional lawyer argued that the realisation of the rule of law was subject to three basic conditions: (1) supremacy of the law as opposed to the arbitrary exercise of executive power; (2) equality of all before the law to be administered by ordinary courts; and (3) judicial protection of individual rights and freedoms.[149]

Because the rule of law stands in frontal opposition to executive orders which express the temporary will of the government, democratic governments are necessarily bound to exercise their power according to clear, stable, and general rules of law, which must therefore be approved by the elected representatives in Parliament and receive proper public scrutiny.

Unfortunately, the Australian legal profession has generally accepted the use of emergency powers by the executive government, thus enabling authorities to issue executive orders that impose heavy fines and imprisonment for non-compliance with certain arbitrary measures. Even the principle of legality is no longer regarded as important by some elements within the judicial elite, at least insofar as the government can allege that an 'emergency' justifies the enactment of measures that profoundly affect the enjoyment of our fundamental rights and freedoms.

In this sense, it might be quite important to consider the role of the legal profession in the legitimisation of totalitarian regimes. The example of Germany in the 1930s provides a good case study. When the Nazis came into power in 1933, the leading lawyer in Germany was Hans Kelsen (1881-1973). Born in Austria and a Jew himself, he was eventually forced out of his position as Dean of Law at the University of Cologne because of the Nazi ascension to power.[150] In the years following World War II, it has been argued that Kelsen's jurisprudential approach might have provided a certain degree of legitimacy to that totalitarian regime. After all, "from the point of view of the science of law", Kelsen himself argued, "the law under the Nazi-government was law. We may regret it but we cannot deny that it was law".[151] As Kelsen also pointed out:

> The legal order of totalitarian states authorizes their governments to confine in concentration camps persons whose opinions, religion, or race they do not like; to force them to perform any kind of labor, even to kill them. Such measures may be morally or violently condemned; but they cannot be considered as taking place outside the legal order of those states.[152]

By proposing a separation of 'is' and 'ought' to the analysis of law, Kelsen contributed to the expulsion of ethics and metaphysics from legal analysis, which ultimately made it quite difficult for the German legal profession to resist the arbitrariness and oppression of the Nazi regime.[153] Kelsen's jurisprudential approach was entirely about revealing the legal system as it stands at a given time, "without legitimising it as just or disqualifying it as unjust; it seeks the real, the positive law, not the right law".[154] However, as Haldemann correctly points out, "the problem of extreme injustice can only be dealt with coherently if we adopt a concept of law that incorporates some basic morality as a limiting criterion".[155]

When one looks at the German legal profession in the 1930s, leaving aside those who were committed to the Nazi ideology, it becomes apparent that legal positivism played a significant role in the failure of lawyers to stand up against the Nazi atrocities. As noted by the late Charles Rice, who served as a Professor of Law at the University of Notre Dame, when the Nazis moved against the Jews, most lawyers who personally opposed the Nazi regime were 'disarmed' by legal positivism.[156] This wouldn't be so if those lawyers had responded to the early Nazi injustices with a sound and principled denunciation rooted in traditional principles of the natural law. However, embedded in the positivist dogma that 'law is law' regardless of its substantive nature, many German lawyers became defenceless against laws of arbitrary or criminal content.[157] Because such lawyers "argued that the evolution of law should be viewed as following purely positive patterns", Seitzer and Thornhill explains, "they concluded that the validity of law depended on its status as an internally consistent set of rules, and it could not be reconstructed or interpreted on the basis of moral prescriptions".[158]

One influential German lawyer who became disarmed by his own positivism was Gustav Radbruch (1878–1949). Once a Justice Minister under the Weimar Republic, Radbruch argued that the government can make any law it pleases so long as it is consistent in enforcing it. Radbruch's legal theory was voluntaristic and identified the validity of law only with its source as opposed to its moral merits. By claiming that, on grounds of social safety, it is critical to always obey the law, Radbruch concluded: "It is the professional duty of the judge to validate the law's claim to validity, to sacrifice his own sense of the right to the authoritative command of the law, to ask only what is legal and not if it is also just."[159]

Radbruch lived long enough to regret having exposed such a legal theory. He witnessed with horror all the atrocities of the Nazi regime. He was appalled by the dramatic effect of Nazi commands and then began to question his own jurisprudential approach. Specifically, Radbruch began to wonder whether his own legal theoretical approach might not have paved the way for the legitimisation of the Nazi regime by not having offered satisfactory limits on the content of legal decisions made through that political process. Ultimately, Radbruch started to believe, as noted by the late Irish jurist, John M. Kelly, that:

> the doctrine that law was whatever a statute said had rendered German justice helpless when confronted with cruelty and injustice once these wore statutory vesture ... In his own reaction and in that of others, Radbruch saw a revival of belief in a transcendent law, however one may like to describe it: the law of God, the law of nature, the law of reason. by which evil positive laws may be condemned as 'legal injustice'. He ended his final lecture by reminding his students that, once upon a time, the title of this course [that is, Legal Philosophy] in the syllabus had been 'The Law of Nature'.[160]

In this sense, in the 1950 edition of his renowned *Rechtsphilosophie*, to the astonishment of his readers Radbruch entirely abandons legal positivism in order to expose a new legal theory which argues that, "where there is not even an attempt at justice, where equality, the core of justice, is deliberately betrayed in the issuance of positive law, the statute is not merely "false law", it lacks completely the very nature of law".[161] Radbruch appeals here to "the natural law or the law of reason". He claims that his new jurisprudential approach has been established "by the work of centuries" and "have come to enjoy such a far-reaching consensus in the declaration of human and civil rights that only the deliberate skeptic can still entertain doubts about some of them".[162] On the basis of these premises, Radbruch then concludes that the commands of the Nazi regime "did not partake of the character of law at all; they were not just wrong law but were no law of any kind".[163] He even provides some examples of 'false' Nazi laws, such as the measures which discriminated against individuals on the basis of biological determinations. Above all, according to the "new" Radbruch, when laws violate the principle of equality and, therefore, our sense of justice, "the people owe them no obedience, and lawyers, too, must find the courage to deny them the character of law".[164]

Of course, legal positivism permitted German lawyers "to rationalise to themselves and others their interpretation and application of laws they might, upon reflection, have considered grotesquely unjust or immoral".[165] "The very dominance of positivist philosophy in Germany had at least seriously inhibited any reaction against the Nazi perversion of legal forms".[166] For example, when the Enabling Act which gave emergency powers to the government was passed by the Reichstag, in March 1933, handing over legislative powers to the Executive for a fixed period of four years, everything was apparently done in accordance with the two-thirds parliamentary majority required by Article 76 of the Weimar Constitution. German constitutional lawyers then rationalised that Germany still had the rule of law (*Rechtsstaat*) because the Executive had obtained its unlimited powers in a constitutional manner. As such, whatever the government decided to do under its emergency powers was regarded as perfectly legal from that strictly positivistic perspective.[167] Hence, the re-enactment of the Enabling Act in 1937, 1939 and 1943 provided "an interesting indication of the regime's schizophrenic combination of legal formalism with ruthless violence and basic contempt for the rule of law".[168]

However, most lawyers in Germany were supportive of Hitler.

These lawyers embraced the notion that Germany was an organic unity, and the spectacle of a divided parliament was unnatural to them. The principal characteristic of German lawyers, including law professors, was illiberalism.[169] The German legal profession generally welcomed Hitler's appointment as Chancellor.[170] In October 1933, in their annual convention at Leipzig, 10,000 lawyers raised their right arms in a Nazi salute and swore, "by the soul of the German people", that they would "strive to follow the course of our Führer to the end of days".[171] On that very day the official journal of the Ministry of Justice exhorted the German legal profession to "march as an army corps of the Führer".[172]

The Reich Minister, Hans Frank (1900-1946), was the head of the German Bar Association (1933–42), the Elected President of the International Chamber of Law (1941–42), and also President of the Academy of German Lawyers. Frank believed that "the basis for the interpretation of all legal sources is the National Socialist ideology that is particularly manifested in the party program and the Führer's statements". According to him, Hitler's will represented the ultimate 'source of the law', thus adding that he belonged to the "greatest lawgivers of universal history". In his 1938 book, Frank stated: "Our constitution is the will of the Führer."[173] As for the role to be played by the judicial elite, Frank commented, it should:

> ... safeguard the concrete order of the racial community, to elimi-nate dangerous elements, to prosecute all acts harmful to the com-munity, and to arbitrate in disagreements between members of the community. The National Socialist ideology, especially as ex-pressed in the Party programme and in the speeches of our Leader, is the basis for interpreting legal sources.[174]

Ironically, the more the members of the legal profession made efforts to legitimise the Nazi regime, the more was the abuse and contempt of the regime towards them. Lawyers who collaborated to the legitimisation of the Nazi regime later were forced to accept the bitter realisation that they were entirely dispensable at the hands of a regime that worked entirely via executive orders and emergency measures, as opposed to the real law. According to the German leader, "the health of the German nation [was] more important than the letter of the law".[175] He did not think much of lawyers, believing they were "men deficient by nature or deformed by experience".[176] In 1942, Hitler revealed his desire to "make every German realize that it is a disgrace to be a lawyer".[177]

German judges were disproportionately supportive of the Nazi regime.[178] They faithfully assisted the Nazis in their goal of achieving unchecked power. In the waning days of the Weimar Republic, those judges openly aligned themselves with the Nazi Party and fully endorsed anti-Semitic sentiments in their judicial rulings.[179] The German judiciary even gave Hitler a very lenient sentence after he was charged with treason following the 1923 Beer Hall Putsch, in Munich.[180] Treason was a serious offence that carried a prison sentence of 20 years' hard labour. However, the presiding judge, Georg Neidhardt, was openly sympathetic to the Nazi cause and gave Hitler unlimited opportunity to speak during his trial. His twenty-four-day trial turned the Nazi leader into a celebrity, capturing headlines around the world. Hitler was given by the judiciary an unlimited chance to make his speeches, and he used colourful language to get his hateful message to all Germany and, for that matter, to the world.[181] Once in power, the Nazis eventually awarded Neidhardt the Presidency of the Bavarian High Court.

Hitler was sentenced for five years but spent only ten months in jail, being released on probation. The Bavarian state prosecutor had opposed his early parole, but the Bavarian Supreme Court had disagreed and ordered his release.[182] From the Landsberg Prison, Hitler found time to write the bible of Nazism, *Mein Kampf*, where he paints himself as a charismatic hero with the mission to save Germany.[183] Hitler was discharged from Landsberg prison on 20 December 1924.

When President Hindenburg died on 2 August 1934, Hitler was confirmed as both Chancellor and the Head of the State. The post of Reich President was abolished. The first step in the plans to consolidate the regime was the 'Nazification' of the court system via the removal of 'undesirable' judges. Jewish judges were immediately dismissed and those of non-Aryan descent forced into retirement. Those who were deemed 'politically unreliable' were also at considerable risk of removal.[184] Judges who remained in office were encouraged to apply the law with respect to contemporary values and principles, and judicial organisations were merged into the Federation of National Socialist Jurists.[185]

The remaining judges happily adapted themselves to the new realities of society.[186] The level of support provided by the judicial elite to the Nazi regime can be testified by the fact that no German judge, with the exception of a small claims judge in Brandenburg-on-the-Havel, resigned in face of the Nazification of the courts.[187] In other words, only one judge in the entire judicial community voluntarily resigned in disapproval during the entire course of the Third Reich.[188] Therefore, wrote Rottleuthner, "the statement that the majority of the judges in the Third Reich at first were diligent on behalf of the new power holders, later probably harassed, but nevertheless submitted, in any case as a body served practically without opposition, cannot be denied".[189]

In March 1933, the Federation of Judges found it appropriate to issue an official declaration expressing their unconditional support of, and cooperation with, the Nazi leadership, "in the revision of German law".[190] The declaration included a 'firm assurance' that those judges would "place their full confidence in the new government".[191] As a result, even some of the most genocidal policies of the Nazi regime were voluntarily initiated and proposed by the judicial elite. Thus in 1933, for example, judge Erich Schultze of the Reich Supreme Court proposed the enactment of a new law criminalising the so-called "betrayal of the race that is … the interbreeding of Germans with members of certain races named by law".[192]

German judges were quite creative in their interpretative approach. They willingly discovered numerous legal possibilities to depriving minority groups, especially the Jews, of their basic human rights, even when no explicit law could be found to justify these decisions.[193] For example, Otto Georg Theirack (1889-1946), the President of the German People's Court, in a 1940 ruling recommended the sending of any individual to concentration camps without the necessity of trial. He argued this would ensure more rapid results, thus avoiding "tedious, very expensive and ponderous court proceedings".[194]

The principal force in the judicial legitimisation of the regime were not the Nazi 'judge-monsters', the likes of Freisler, Rothaug and Theirack, but instead the so-called 'good' judges who did not have enough courage to question the Nazi atrocities and gross violations of human rights.[195] By not questioning the validity of Nazi rules these judges provided the façade of legal normality to the totalitarian regime. By the end of World War II, such judges were indicted in the Nuremberg Trials for assisting in the commitment of war crimes and crimes against humanity. These judges appealed to narrow legal positivism although they failed even to apply the Weimar Constitution as an *ex post facto* attempt to "wash their hands in the waters of legal theory'"[196] Be as it may, those judges miserably "failed to perform as ethical paragons for the population at large. They acted as 'yes-men' to a brutal regime. Instead of leading in the field of at least intellectual resistance to a criminal state; they readily joined it as followers, and in quite a few instances as activists.[197]

The same attitude of subservience happened amongst academic lawyers. One reason as to why professors of law were so willing to uphold the Nazi regime was their opposition to natural law theory and consequent denial of the inalienable rights of the individual. In the early 1930s the most influential German academic lawyer was undoubtedly Hans Kelsen (1881–1973). Kelsen was a legal theorist who confined his scholarly legal analysis to a theory of the positive law and its interpretation. He was anxious to explain the difference, even the contrast, between what is *just* and what is *legal*. But Kelsen himself admitted that this separation of justice and law did not exist in German-speaking nations until the rise of legal historicism in the mid-19th century. Prior to legal historicism, Kelsen explained, "the question of justice was considered its fundamental problem by juridical science".[198]

The leading German historicist, Friedrich Carl von Savigny (1779-1861), was a towering figure amongst the legal elite and holds "a status in German legal science not dissimilar to that of Johann Wolfgang von Goethe (1749–1832) in German literature".[199] Savigny believed in the organic evolution on the law and, in one of his most influential books, entitled *On the Vocation of Our Age for Legislation and Jurisprudence*, the concept of inalienable rights of the individual is described as too abstract and a mere doctrine of 18th-century Enlightenment.

Savigny believed that the individual is no more than a member of the collective body as much as each age of the nation is the continuation of all past ages. History is treated not as a source of example and tradition but the path that leads to the "true knowledge of our own condition".[200] Accordingly, law is approached as something that needs to adapt itself to the contemporary needs of society, so that conflicting arguments can be decided in accordance with the commands of the State. As a result, German lawyers were no longer interested in the protection of individual rights "but the sovereignty of the State, a product of German philosophical pantheism".[201] This is how Hans Gerber described the new spirit of German law after 1933: "National Socialism insists that justice is not a system of abstract and autonomous values such as the various types of Natural Law systems. Each society has its own concept of justice."[202] Ultimately, writes Richard Overy, the historicist rejection of objective legal standards,

> ... made law historically contingent, a product of its own time and place ... Law was regarded not set in stone but something that evolved and changed with altered historical circumstances. Historical reality, it was argued, dictated the nature of legal systems and governed their moral worth. ... In the Third Reich the highest justice was the preservation of the life of the nation; the nation was the source of law; hence law was also just.[203]

German legal historicism thus became the driving force behind the promotion of the Aryan racial myth.[204] The idea that fundamental rights could impose moral obligations on the State was discarded as a product of 'bourgeois liberalism'. Since the legal historicist thesis was that justice is entirely conventional and ultimately determined by the State, the result was not just legal positivism but also moral nihilism. The primary difficulty with this sort of historicism, wrote Leo Strauss, "is that all societies have their ideals, cannibal society no less than civilized ones ... If principles are sufficiently justified by the fact that they are accepted by a society, the principles of cannibalism are as defensible or sound as those of civilized life".[205]

Nazi legislation and case law showed a remarkable similarity with the doctrines of German legal historicism. Legal standards were deemed subjective in character and there was no room for personal choices apart from the choices explicitly made by those in power.[206] There was an elusive, romantic-mystical notion of the *Volksgeist*, which was not attached to the German individual, because "a real people would not itself have any practical law-making power as an expression of its common consciousness, which was then indeed the case in Nazi Germany".[207] This gradual process of homogenisation 'assimilated' the individual into the organic body of the Nazi State.[208]

It is understood the threat of punishment or the fear of losing their jobs was not the main reason the legal profession supported the Nazi regime. Academic journal articles by leading law professors, for example, "displayed a colourful mix of irrational fantasies, self-debasing declarations of submission, and traditional dogmatic jurisprudence with a ready (positivist) acceptance of the new legal order".[209] These articles were entirely dismissive of the idea of individual rights as a concept regarded by these academic lawyers as "a degenerate form of bourgeois constitutionalism".[210] Thus Dr Freisler, a legal academic who taught jurisprudence at the University of Berlin, stated: "Fundamental rights which create free spheres for individuals untouchable by the state are irreconcilable with the totalitarian principle of the new state".[211]

Under the influence of these academic lawyers, it is not surprising that law students provided the chief manpower reservoir of Nazi extremism. The Nazis did consistently well among those law students who saw Nazism as an exciting radical movement. They liked its egalitarianism, and they liked its anti-Semitism too. Indeed, those students were more anti-Semitic than either the working class or the bourgeoisie.[212]

In October 1933, 'racial laws' became the main topic of discussion during the annual conference of German law professors.[213] Its keynote speaker, law professor Helmut Nicolai (1895–1955), was co-author of a well-known academic book entitled *Rassengesetzliche Rechtslehre* (1921). Professor Nicolai spoke with great enthusiasm about the enactment of 'racial laws', which, according to him, would help Germans to enjoy the proper 'blood inheritance'.[214] According to him, the 'pure conscience' of such laws' 'creative spirit' would 'retroactively' endorse the ancient qualities of the Germanic law.[215]

Even before the regime was consolidated, the Nazis had already proposed in the Reichstag a law which determined that persons of certain physical or mental defects should be exterminated. Once in power they enacted laws which claimed the lives of thousands of individuals. The extermination of thousands did not disturb the conscience of the legal community, which overall supported eugenics. In 1920, a lawyer called Karl Binding (1841–1930) had already co-authored an influential book that bluntly dismissed the possibility of medical misdiagnosis being a matter of concern, even if it eventually resulted in the elimination of human life. Binding stated: "For family members the loss is naturally very severe, but the human race loses so many members to errors that one more or less hardly matters."[216]

If one considers the 84 names to be found on the 1922 membership list of the Association of Constitutional Lawyers, academic legal positivists were not surprisingly the largest and most influential group. Alongside the positivists, as a second most influential group, were legal historicists such as Rudolf Smend (1882–1975), who linked the legitimacy of the State with its capacity to generate national cohesion.[217] Smend and other constitutional historicists shared with the positivists a disregard for liberal constitutionalism, including the idea of constitutional rights and the doctrine of separation of powers. In conformity with the concept of *Volks-Nomos* ('people-norm'), those constitutional lawyers denied the existence of individual rights against the State. In sum, they believed that the object of the law "was no longer to check but rather to encourage arbitrary exertion of public power".[218] Such interpretations by highly esteemed legal academics, writes Kershaw, "were of inestimable value in legitimating a form of domination which ... effectively undermined the rule of law in favour of arbitrary exercise of political will".[219]

The leading Nazi jurist, Carl Schmitt (1888-1985), owed his first academic appointment at the University of Cologne thanks to the efforts of Kelsen.[220] Schmitt joined the Nazi Party in May 1933, and was immediately appointed Dean of Law at the University of Berlin. He argued that liberal conceptualisations of the rule of law (*Rechtsstaat*) reflected the 'self-deceiving' and 'weak-spirited' tendencies found in liberal democracy.[221] A severe critic of the Weimar Republic, he argued its constitution did not provide the kind of 'strong government' the nation required. Despite Schmitt's apparent aversion to positivism, his main argument, that the legal system is contingent and subject to the will of the sovereign, does not contradict the positive command-theory of law. On the contrary, Schmitt's primary claim that the validity of the law is not primarily justified on moral grounds effectively places him in the solid camp of legal positivism, at least in respect to the classical positivist understanding of the correlation between political will and the validity of the law. Schmitt believed that legal matters are inevitably subject to political contingency, so that the legitimacy of the law is not determined by universal ethical standards. He objectively endorsed the primary positivist claim that "law obtains legitimacy simply because of the fact that it has evolved into a certain positive form and that, supported by a state apparatus, it provides a concrete order of norms that shape and structure social expectations".[222]

The Nazis were political agitators who knew very well how to exacerbate popular resentments by appealing to irrational sentiments. As noted by Laurence Rees, "it is almost impossible to overestimate the importance of enemies to Adolf Hitler. Enemies did not just feed the hatred he had felt at much of the world since his earliest years but provided a much-needed bounding element for the first supporters of the Nazi party".[223] Schmitt was useful in this respect because he had in his philosophical writings described the concept of 'enmity' as the most defining quality of politics. In the 1920s he developed a theory which legitimised these base sentiments by arguing that law and morals are the end products of the struggle between inimical groups for political supremacy. According to Schmitt,

> The specifically political distinction underpinning political actions and motives is that between friend and foe. It corresponds in the realm of politics to the relatively independent contrasts in other realms: between good and evil in ethics, the beautiful and ugly in aesthetics, and so on. The [distinction between friend and foe] is self-sufficient – that is, it neither derives from one or more of these contrasts nor is reduced to them ... [I]t can exist, both in theory and practice, without the concurrent application of other distinctions – moral, aesthetic, economic, and so on. The political enemy need not be morally evil or aesthetically ugly; he need not appear as an economic competitor, and it may even be very advantageous to do business with him. But he is the other, the stranger; and it is enough he is, in an especially intensive existential sense, someone different and alien, so that, in the event of a conflict, he represents the negation of one's own being, and for that reason must be resisted and fought in order to protect one's self-like (seinmässig) life-style.[224]

Schmitt actively collaborated with the Nazi regime between 1933 and 1936. Over that period, he authored articles that supported emergency powers that authorised the government to suspend constitutional rights and freedoms. Under Article 48 of the Weimar Constitution, the President of the German Republic was authorised to rule by decree during times of emergency.[225] Following the burning of the Reichstag on 27 February 1933, President Hindenburg relied on emergency powers provisions to sign into law the notorious Reichstag Fire Decree.[226] Schmitt argued that this executive order provided extraordinary powers that were in principle devoid of any constitutional limits. This executive order suspended the basic right of the individual as set out in the Weimar Constitution, thus granting the national, Reich

Cabinet, the power to enact laws which were deemed necessary for the protection of the German people.[227] What followed was the complete loss of individual rights as these were suspended 'until further notice'.[228] For Schmitt, such suspension of rights was perfectly valid because, in his *Political Theology*, a book published in 1922, he had already explained that, in his opinion,

> The nature of state authority is revealed most clearly in the state of emergency. Here the decision making and the legal norm diverge, and ... authority proves that it need not have a basis in law in order to establish justice'. Once this state of emergency has been declared, it is clear that the constituted authority of the state continues to exist ... [and] the law is placed in abeyance ... The decision exempts that authority from every normative restraint and renders it absolute in the true sense of the word. In a state of emergency, the constituted authority suspends the law on the basis of the right to protect its own existence.[229]

The 'legalised arbitrariness' envisaged by the Nazi leadership was entirely justified on the ground of the regular re-enactment of emergency powers. The *ex post facto* Acts of July 1934, which happened between 30 June and 2 July 1934, were carried out under these emergency powers. The *Night of the Long Knives*, as the episode came to be known, can be explained as a series of political assassinations of Nazi figures associated with the *Sturmabteilung* (SA), the paramilitary Nazi Brownshirts. At least 85 people died as a result of the crackdown, including the SA leader Ernst Röhm.[230] Hitler took personal responsibility for these assassinations and told the Reichstag: "If anyone reproaches me and asks why I did not resort to the regular courts of justice, then all I can say is this: in this hour I was responsible for the fate of the German people."[231]

Although these people were executed arbitrarily and without due process, the Night of the Long Knives did not really bother the legal profession. In fact, some lawyers like Carl Schmitt went as far as to provide legal justification for the killings. Hence, on 3

July 1934, a law concerning the self-preservation of the nation was enacted retrospectively, which stated that 'the measures taken on June 30, July 1 and 2, in order to suppress reasonable attacks, are declared legal.'[232] This meant that the regime could now be placed above the law. Schmitt, however, qualified that executive order as a "genuine jurisdiction not subject to justice but supreme justice in itself ... Law is no longer an objective norm but a spontaneous emanation of the Führer's will".[233]

When Schmitt fell out of favour with the Nazi Leadership, he attempted to regain their confidence by authoring legal articles supporting the expansion of the German national borders. From 1936 to 1945 Schmitt devoted most of his legal academic work to the area of public international law. Thus, he developed the concept of the *Grossraum* or 'large area', which served to give legal justification for the expansion of German territory eastwards, and to subject and enslave the population of neighbouring nations. This concept of *Grossraum* was strongly associated with the notorious *Lebensraum*, or 'living space' theory, in which the Nazis contended that life could be resumed as a constant struggle between the different races for 'living space'.[234]

As can be seen, the atrocities committed by the Nazi regime cannot be isolated, like some sort of mere accident, from the prevailing philosophy of the powerful German legal profession. German lawyers were eager, even anxious, to legitimise a brutal regime which denied any 'inalienable right' of the individual against the all-powerful State. Those lawyers were hostile to liberal principles of the rule of law and generally welcomed the Nazi regime, in 1933. In many respects, lawyers played a decisive role in the decline of justice and equality in 1930s Germany.

To conclude, the contributions of the German legal profession were of inestimable value in the legitimisation of the Nazi regime. The German legal profession provided justification for the murderous actions of that regime, which otherwise would have been recognised as unlawful and devoid of constitutionality. Above all, the German legal profession supported the use of emergency powers that facilitated the ultimate denial of ethics and metaphysics in conceptualisations of the law, which eventually resulted in a lack of legal basis for lawful resistance against that totalitarian regime.

There is no doubt that Australia, now that it has embarked on rule by health decree, would be able to learn from this dreadful episode of German history.

9

A SOBERING REFLECTION

Australian governments have decided that the unvaccinated will be treated differently to the vaccinated. In practice, this means that the unvaccinated have less rights to work, less freedoms to travel, or even to visit friends and relatives under certain circumstances.

One of the primary goals of the judicial function is to protect citizens against any adverse impact on their enjoyment of fundamental legal rights, including freedom of choice, freedom of movement, and freedom of association. In the *Australian Capital Television* case, in 1992, Justice Gaudron referred to "a free society governed in accordance with the principles of representative parliamentary democracy" as entailing "freedom of movement, freedom of association and freedom of speech".

Because the Constitution prohibits any form of compulsion subjecting citizens to medical or pharmaceutical services, including mandatory vaccination, any legislation that requires compulsory vaccination, either directly or indirectly, constitutes a form of civil conscription that is constitutionally invalid. We should have no doubt that "vaccine passport restrictions" unconstitutionally impinge on the democratic principle of equality before the law and the free movement of citizens within their own country.

The jurisprudence of the High Court indicates that the prohibition of civil conscription must be construed widely to invalidate any law requiring such conscription expressly or by practical implication. From a constitutional point of view, as we have explained in this book, the jurisprudence of the High Court indicates that what cannot be done directly, cannot be achieved indirectly without violating section 51 of the Constitution. This point is addressed by Justice Webb in *British Medical Association v Commonwealth*:

> If Parliament cannot lawfully do this directly by legal means **it cannot lawfully do it indirectly** by creating a situation, as distinct from merely taking advantage of one, in which the individual is left no real choice but compliance" (emphasis added).[235]

It is elementary that Australia's political class has equally violated important principles of international law. International human rights legislation explicitly prohibits the removal of non-derogable rights, even in situations of an alleged "emergency". This prohibition encompasses any form of compulsion which exposes individuals to mandatory vaccination. In summary, any Australian law that requires vaccine mandates either directly or indirectly, is not only constitutionally invalid, but it also constitutes a violation of Australia's obligations under public international law.[236]

More fundamentally, it is entirely self-evident that Australians are endowed with constitutional protections as derived from the notion exposed by the Court of "a free society governed in accordance with the principles of democratic parliamentary government".

With the financial support (and enablement) of their federal counterpart, the State Premiers often express a desire to extend these emergency powers for a further period. We may be repeating history as the desire to extend emergency powers appears to confirm the worst fears of the Austrian-British economist and philosopher Friedrich Hayek. In *Law, Legislation and Liberty* (1981), this Nobel Prize laureate commented that emergency powers always have their way of becoming more permanent. Hayek offered this sobering reflection:

> The conditions under which such emergency powers may be granted without creating the danger that they will be retained when the absolute necessity has passed are among the most difficult and important points a constitution must decide on. *'Emergencies' have always been the pretext on which the safeguards* of individual liberty have been eroded – and once they are suspended it is not difficult for anyone who has assumed such emergency powers to see to it that the emergency will persist.[237]

As argued in the previous chapter, this is not entirely dissimilar to what happened in 1930s' Germany. There, a notorious chancellor also turned his emergency powers into more permanent ones. This correlation between the instrument used by that German government to continue ruling arbitrarily and what the Australian political class is presently doing is, quite frankly, strikingly similar. This undeniable fact has been vividly manifested, among others, in the constant renewal of emergency powers that violate the rule of law and disregard the most elementary rights of the citizen.

It is particularly important to be reminded of how dictatorial regimes are normally brought into existence. There is always an 'emergency' which can be used to justify the violation of fundamental rights. Of course, we are not comparing the current use of emergency powers in Australia with the use that was made of similar instruments in 1930s' Germany. However, we are effectively stating here an undeniable truth: that such instruments of extraordinary power have always been used as a means of suppressing fundamental rights and dramatically increasing the power of the State.

The rise of totalitarianism in Europe in the 1930s cannot be considered an isolated fact, as some sort of 'accident'. In those days, the Germans were quite willing, even anxious, to be protected by a powerful government. They willingly renounced their freedoms and preferred to be ruled by a government that was powerful enough to protect them from any real or imaginary threat. Unfortunately, their trusted political rulers led the nation to a disastrous military conflict at the cost of 75 million deaths. Germany alone sustained 8 million losses, including 3 million civilians who died through massacres, mass-bombings, disease, and starvation.[238]

Obviously, it would be preposterous to conclude that Australia is facing similar charges. However, the use of emergency powers in Australia certainly results in the abuse of power by arbitrary measures that profoundly undermine the rule of law; this can become more permanent in time. Presently, Australian authorities are enacting measures that consolidate statism and allow informers to assist authorities in tracing and incarcerating citizens without warrants on the grounds of prospective conduct. Any person in this country can now be arrested when the authority assumes that they have failed to comply with these directions. As such, basic legal principles inherited from the common law and our tradition of constitutional government (including due process and recourse to the writ of habeas corpus) are seriously undermined.

Australians have passively watched their governments use a broad range of extra-constitutional powers to control almost every single aspect of their lives. These governments have acquired emergency powers that entitle public officials to detain citizens, search their premises without a warrant, and even force entire populations into lockdowns once this might be deemed necessary to protect the public health. Under this context, governments can detain citizens who refuse or fail to comply with their directions.[239] They will be detained by the authorities and no legal remedy will be made available. As Ian Hanke pointed out:

> These extraordinary powers are arbitrary and extreme. They are a draconian attack on civil liberties the like of which Australia has never seen before. Further because all laws are overridden there would appear to be little recourse to any excesses by an authorised officer or their civilians co-opted by them. These laws are so broad and ill-defined that you could be detained for almost anything.[240]

Thomas Jefferson once famously stated: "A government big enough to give you everything you want, is strong enough to take everything you have". And Benjamin Franklin, another leading figure of early American history, added: "Those who would give up essential liberty to purchase a little temporary safety, deserve neither liberty nor safety".[241] Franklin was urging his people to not abandon their basic freedoms in exchange for a false sense of security. What is happening in Australia is profoundly tragic. John Locke famously argued that governments have no other end "but the preservation of these rights, and therefore can never have a right to destroy, enslave, or designedly to impoverish the subjects". The Australian people have a lawful right to resist and to demand the full restoration of their basic rights and freedoms. We can only hope that the High Court will be willing to assist the people in the process.

Notes

1   The Great Barrington Declaration is available at: https://gbdeclaration.org/.

2   Ashley Sadler, 'Clinical psychologist warns of totalitarianism, atrocity resulting from mass COVID buy-in', LifeSiteNews, 10 December 2021.

3   (1909) 8 CLR 330.

4   Suri Ratnapala, *Welfare State or Constitutional State?* (Sydney: Centre for Independent Studies, 1990), 19.

5   O. H. Phillips and P. Johnson, *O Hood Phillips' Constitutional and Administrative Law*, (Sweet & Maxwell, 1987), 33.

6   Adriaan Bedner and Jacqueline A.C. Vel, 'An Analytical Framework for Empirical Research on Access to Justice' (2010) 1. *The Journal of Law, Social Justice and Global Development*, 1, 21.

7   St Thomas Aquinas, *De Regimine Principum* Bk I, Ch 2 (tr. Gerald B. Phelan, Sheed & Ward, 1938), 55.

8   T R S Allan, *Law, Liberty, and Justice: The Legal Foundations of British Constitutionalism,* (Clarendon Press, 1993), 21.

9   T.R.S. Allan, 'Freedom, Equality, Legality', in James R. Silkenat et al (eds.), *The Legal Doctrines of the Rule of Law and the Legal State* (Rechtsstaat) (Springer, 2014), 155.

10 T. R. S. Allan, *Constitutional Justice: A Liberal Theory of the 'rule of law'* (Oxford University Press, Oxford, 2001), 2.

11 Allan, above n 9, 44.

12 Ibid., 21-2.

13 R. C. van Caenegem, *An Historical Introduction to Western Constitutional Law* (Cambridge University Press, 1995), 15.

14 E. Böckenförde, *State, Society and Liberty: Studies in Political Theory and Constitutional Law* (Berg, 1991), 50.

15 Phillips et al, above n 5, 36.

16   A.V. Dicey, *Introduction to the Study of the Law of the Constitution* [1886] (Liberty Fund, 1982) 120-122.

17   Ibid. 123.

18   Benjamin Constant, *Political Writings* (Cambridge University Press, 1988) 195.

19   John Locke, *Second Treatise on Civil Government* [1689] Section 135.

20   T. R. S. Allan, *Law, Liberty, and Justice: The Legal Foundations of British Constitutionalism,* (Clarendon Press, 1993), 21.

21   Ibid.

22   Mortimer N.S. Sellers, 'What Is the Rule of Law and Why Is It So Important?', in James R. Silkenat et al (eds.), *The Legal Doctrines of the Rule of Law and the Legal State* (Rechtsstaat) (Springer, 2014) 4.

23   Mortimer N.S. Sellers, 'What Is the Rule of Law and Why Is It So Important?', in James R. Silkenat et al (eds.), *The Legal Doctrines of the Rule of Law and the Legal State* (Rechtsstaat) (Springer, 2014) 6.

24   Robin Charlow, 'American Constitutional Analysis and a Substantive Understanding of the Rule of Law', in James R. Silkenat et al (eds.), T*he Legal Doctrines of the Rule of Law and the Legal State* (Rechtsstaat) (Springer, 2014) 253.

25   Philip Selznick, 'Legal Cultures and the 'rule of law'' in M Krygier and A Czarnota (eds), *The 'Rule of Law' After Communism* (Ashgate, Dartmouth, 1999) 37. Selznick was professor of sociology and law at the University of California, Berkeley.

26   Martin Krygier, *False Dichotomies, True Perplexities, and the Rule of Law. Paper presented at the Center for the Study of Law and Society,* University of California-Berkeley, 2003, 11.

27   Martin Krygier, 'Rule of Law' in N.J. Smelse and P.B. Baltes (eds.), *International Enclylopedia of the Social & Behavioral Sciences* (2001), 13404.

28   Martin Krygier, 'Compared to What? Thoughts on Law and Justice', *Quadrant Magazine,* December 1993.

29   Martin Krygier, 'The Rule of Law: An Abuser's Guide'. Paper presented at the 13th annual conference on 'The Individual vs The State', Central European University, Budapest, Hungary, 10-11 June 2004, 23.

30 Friedrich A. Hayek, *The Constitution of Liberty* (The University of Chicago Press, 1960) 205.

31 Brian Z. Tamanaha, *A General Jurisprudence of Law and Society* (Oxford University Press, 2001) 140.

32 Max Weber, *Theory of Social and Economic Organization* (New York: Praeger, 1983) 215.

33 Sir Ivor Jennings, *The Law and the Constitution* (London: University of London Press, 1959) 46.

34 Lawrence M. Friedman, *The Legal System: A Social Science Perspective* (New York/NY: Russell Sage, 1975) 193-94.

35 Miguel Schor, 'Constitutionalism Through the Looking Glass of Latin America' (2006) 41, *Texas International Law Journal* 1, 7.

36 Ibid.

37 M.C.J. Vile, *Constitutionalism and the Separation of Powers* (2nd ed., Indianapolis/IN: Liberty Fund, 1998) 261

38 Brian Z. Tamanaha, *On The Rule of Law: History, Politics, Theory* (Cambridge University Press, 2004) 35.

39 Suri Ratnapala, 'Sri Lanka at the Constitutional Crossroads: Gaullist Presidentialism, Westminster Democracy or Tripartite Separation of Powers' (2003/2004) *LAWASIA Journal* 33, 55.

40 (1931) 46 CLR 73.

41 Ratnapala, above n 39.

42 Patrick O'Brien, 'The Real Politics of the West Australian Constitution and the Executive State', in: Patrick O'Brian and Martyn Webb, *The Executive State: WA Inc. & The Constitution* (Constitutional Press, 1991) 2.

43 Nicholas Aroney, 'Bicameralism and Representations of Democracy', in: Nicholas Aroney, Scott Presser, and J R Nethercote (eds.), *Restraining Elective Dictatorship* (University of Western Australia Press, 2008) 29.

44 Martyn Webb, 'Sovereigns not Subjects: Toward New Constitutions for the Australian States', in: Patrick O'Brian and Martyn Webb, *The Executive State: WA Inc. & The Constitution* (Constitutional Press, 1991) 112.

45 Montesquieu, Bk. 2, Chap I.

46 Ibid, Bk2, Chap 9.

47 Suri Ratnapala, 'Sri Lanka at the Constitutional Crossroads: Gaullist Presidentialism, Westminster Democracy or Tripartite Separation of Powers' [2003/2004] LAWSIA Journal 33, 54. See also: Augusto Zimmermann & Lorraine Finlay, 'Suri Ratnapala's Contribution to the Understanding of the Rule of Law' (2014) 33 (2) *University of Queensland Law Journal* 367, 368-72.

48 Ratnapala, above n 47, 49.

49 Caroline Schelle, 'COVID-19 Victoria: Anti-vaccine protesters rallied in Melbourne's CBD over coronavirus vaccine mandates', News.com.au, November 6, 2021.

50 Suri Ratnapala, *Australian Constitutional Law: Foundations and Theory* (Oxford University Press, 2002), 7.

51 C.L. Ten, 'Constitutionalism and The 'rule of law'', R.E. Goodwin and P. Pettit (eds.), *A Companion to Contemporary Political Philosophy* (Cambridge/MA: Blackwell: 1993). Chin Liew Ten is Emeritus Professor of Philosophy and former Head of the Philosophy Department at the National University of Singapore.

52 (1992) 177 CLR 106, at 212 (Gaudron J.)

53 (1992) 177 CLR 1, at 48 (Brennan J.)

54 Ibid.

55 Giovanni Sartori, 'Constitutionalism: A Preliminary Discussion' (1962) 56, *American Political Science Review*, 853., 861.

56 Murray Gleeson, *The Rule of Law and he Constitution* (ABC Books, Sydney, 2000), 67-68.

57 See: Alexandra Private Geriatric Hospital Pty Ltd v Commonwealth (1987) 162 CLR 271, at 279; 69 ALR 631; Halliday v Commonwealth (2000) 45 ATR 458; [2000] FCA 950 at [11].

58 AAP FactCheck, 'Does a constitutional clause ban vaccine mandates in Australia?', July 26, 2021.

59 [2021] NSWSC 1320

60 At [275]

61 (2009) 236 CLR 573.

62 Ibid at [151].

63 (1949) 79 CLR 201; [1949] HCA 44.

64 (1949) 79 CLR 201, at 287 (Williams J).

65   (2009) 236 CLR 573

66   Ibid at [62].

67   (1949) 79 CLR 201, at 295 (Webb J).

68   *Bowater v Rowley Regis Corp* [1944] KB 476, at 479 (Scott LJ).

69   Email message from John Duval to A. Zimmermann, dated 9 December 2021.

70   (1949) 79 CLR 201, at 293 (Webb J).

71   (1992) 174 CLR 455.

72   Ibid at [8].

73   Airdale National Health Service Trust v Bland [1993] AC 789, at 889. (Mustill LJ). Similarly, in that same case Lord Judge Goff remarked at 866:

> [I]t is established that the principle of self-determination requires that respect must be given to the wishes of the patient, so that, if an adult patient of sound mind refuses, however unreasonably, to consent to treatment or care by which his life would or might be prolonged, the doctors responsible for his care must give effect to his wishes, even though they do not consider it to be in his best interests to do so: To this extent, the principle of sanctity of human life must yield to the principle of self-determination.

74   'Statement by Mrs Franklin D Roosevelt', Department of State Bulletin (December 1948) 751. Quoted in Ngaire Naffine, *Law's Meaning of Life: Philosophy, Religion, Darwin and the Legal Person* (Hart Publishing: Oxford, 2009), 103.

75   AAP FactCheck, 'The Nuremberg Code doesn't apply to COVID-19 vaccinations', 9 June 2021.

76   Kasen K Riemersma et al., 'Vaccinated and Unvaccinated Individuals Have a Similar Viral Loads in Communities with a High Prevalence of the SARS-CoV-2 Delta Variant', *MedRxiv*, July 31, 2021.

77   Adam Taylor, 'Blood clot risks: Comparing AstraZeneca vaccine and the contraceptive pill', The Conversation, April 10, 2021.

78   Emily Craig, 'Blood in their Hands': UK Fury at EU Leaders for Slating AstraZeneca's Covid Vaccine 'Out of Spite Over Brexit' After Study Finds It has The Same Risk of Blood Clots as Pfizer's', *Daily Mail*, 29 July 2021.

79   Rocco Loiacono, 'Most Covid patients at Israeli hospital fully vaccinated? What does this mean for Australia?' *The Spectator,* August 12, 2021.

80   'Australia's Vaccine Agreements', Australian Government, Department of Health, available online, last updated: 14 December 2021)

81   'COVID-19 Vaccine: Provisional Registrations', Australian Government, Department of Health, Therapeutic and Goods Administration', available online, last visited: 16 December 2021.

82   The Hon Greg Hunt, 'Interview with David Speers on ABC Insiders on the COVID-19 Vaccine Rollout', Government of Australia, Department of Health, 21 February 2021.

83   'Is it True? Were COVID-19 Vaccines Rushed Through Approvals or Given Emergency Use Authorisations in Australia?', Australian Government, Department of Health, 25 August 2021.

84   Stephen Chavura, Facebook, available at https://www.facebook. com/stephen.chavura.

85   James Grierson, Rowena Mason, Peter Walker, Andrew Gregory and Linda Geddes, 'UK's Minimum Gap for Covid Booster Jabs to be Halved to Three Months', *The Guardian,* 30 November 2021.

86   E. Bendavid et al., 'COVID-19 Antibody Seroprevalence in Santa Clara country, California', Stanford University, 11 April 2020.

87   John P.A. Ionnidis, 'A Fiasco in the Making? As the Coronavirus Pandemic Takes Hold, We Are Making Decisions Without Reliable Data', Statnews, 17 March 2020.

88   'Australia Vaccinating Children Against COVID-19 From Early Next Year', Australian Government, Department of Health, 10 December 2021.

89   'Covid: Children's Extremely Low Risk Confirmed by Study', BBC News, 9 July 2021. See also: Erika Molteni et al, 'Illness Duration and Symptom Profile in Symptomatic UK School-Age Children Tested for SARS-CoV-2', The Lancet – Children and Adolescent Health, August 03, 2021.

90   Ibid.

91   'JCVI Staement on COVID-19 Vaccination of Children and Young People Aged 12 to 17 Years: 15 July 2021', UK Department of Health & Social Care, 19 July 2021.

92   Ronald N. Kostoff, Daniela Calina, Andrey A Svistunov, Aristidis Tastsakis et al., 'Why Are We Vaccinating Children Against COVID-19?' (2021) *Toxicology Reports*, 1665-1684.

93   David Bell and Roland Salmon, 'Public Health Logic of COVID-19 Vaccinations', *The British Medical Journal*, 6 September 2021. See also: "Covid-19: JCVI Opts Not to Recommend Universal Vaccination of 12-15 Year Olds', *The British Medical Journal,* 03 September 2021.

94   Available at https://www.qld.gov.au/health/conditions/health-alerts/coronavirus-COVID-19/current-status/queensland-restrictions-update/public-health-and-social-measures-linked-to-vaccination-status.

95   "The first thing to be stressed about s 51(xxix) of the Constitution for the purposes of the present case is that its reference to "external affairs" is unqualified. The paragraph does not refer to "Australia's external affairs". Nor does it limit the subject matter of the grant of power to external affairs which have some especial connection with Australia. The words "external" means "outside". As a matter of language, it carries no implication beyond that of location. The word "affairs" has a wide and indefinite meaning. It is appropriate to refer to relations, matters or things. Used without qualification or limitation, the phrase "external affairs" is appropriate, in a constitutional grant of legislative power, encompass both relationships and things: relationships with or between foreign States and foreign or international organizations or other entities; matters or things which are territorially external to Australia regardless of whether they have some identified connection with Australia or whether they be the subject matter of international treaties, dealings, rights or obligations. Such a construction of the phrase "external affairs" in s 51(xxix) is supported by the settled principle of constitutional construction which requires that, subject to any express or implied general constitutional limitations and any overriding restrictions flowing from express or implied constitutional guarantees, the grants of legislative power contained in s 51 be (sic) construed with all the generality which the words used admit and be given their full force and effect". – *Polyukhovich v The Commonwealth* (the War Crimes case) (1991) 172 CLR 501 [599] (Deane J). For a general overview of the external affairs power, see Gabriël A Moens and John Trone, *The Constitution of the* Commonwealth of Australia Annotated, 9th ed (LexisNexis Butterworths, Australia, 2016), 185-193.

96   Bede Harris, *Essential Constitutional Law* (Sydney: Cavendish,

2000), 136.

97   Sir Harry Gibbs, 'The Decline of Federalism?' (1994) 18
      University of Queensland Law Journal 1, 4-5.

98   Ibid.

99   A. Stewart and G. Williams, *Work Choices: What the High Court
      Said* (Sydney: Federation Press, 2007), 10

100   The external affairs power, of course, encompasses more than
      simply the power to legislate domestically to incorporate the terms
      of international treaties. It also provides the Commonwealth
      government with the constitutional power to introduce legislation
      dealing with Australia's relations with other countries: *R v
      Sharkey* [1949] HCA 46; (1949) 79 CLR 121; *Kirmani v Captain
      Cook Cruises Pty Ltd* (No 1) [1985] HCA 8; (1985) 159 CLR 351,
      and relating to matters or things geographically situated outside
      Australia: *Polyukhovich v Commonwealth* [1991] HCA 32; (1991)
      172 CLR 501; *XYZ v Commonwealth* [2006] HCA 25; (2006) 227
      CLR 532).

      Section 18C of the *Racial Discrimination Act* 1975 (Cth) is not
      a law with regards to the subject of relations between Australia
      and other governments and does not fall within the scope of the
      geographic externality principle. The final possible basis for the
      operation of the external affairs power is in relation to laws with
      respect to 'a matter of international concern': *Polyukhovich v
      Commonwealth* [1991] HCA 32; (1991) 172 CLR 501, 560-561
      (Brennan J); *Koowarta v Bjelke-Petersen* [1982] HCA 27; (1982)
      153 CLR 168, 220 (Stephen J) ('*Koowarta*'). This doctrine has
      not, however, been definitively accepted by the High Court as
      providing a valid constitutional basis for domestic legislation,
      being instead referred to as 'an undeveloped concept': *XYZ
      v Commonwealth* [2006] HCA 25; (2006) 227 CLR 532, 575
      [127] (Kirby J) that gives rise to 'immense difficulties': *XYZ v
      Commonwealth* [2006] HCA 25; (2006) 227 CLR 532, 612 [225]
      (Callinan and Heydon JJ).

101   *Commonwealth v Tasmania* [1983] HCA 21; (1983) 158 CLR 1
      ('Tasmanian Dam Case').

102   Ibid 125 (Mason J).

103   [2009] HCA 23; (2009) 238 CLR 1, 162 (Heydon J) ('Pape').

104   Janine Graham, 'The Informer: 'Seriously, One More Comment
      About Human Rights...', Says Daniel Andrews', *The Canberra
      Times*, 27 July 2020.

105 United Nations Economic and Social Council, United Nations Sub-Commission on Prevention of Discrimination and Protection of Minorities, Siracusa Principles on the Limitation and Derogation of Provisions in the International Covenant on Civil and Political Rights, Annex, UN Doc E/CN.4/ (1984) [58].

106 Rocco Loiacono, 'Most Covid patients at Israeli hospital fully vaccinated? What does this mean for Australia?' *The Spectator*, August 12, 2021.

107 'Right to Health: Public Sector Guidance Sheet', Australian Government, Attorney-General Department.

108 U.N. Economic and Social Council – Committee on Economic, Social and Cultural Rights, General Comment No.14. (11 August 2000)

109 Ibid.

110 Ibid.

111 (1949) 79 CLR 201, at 293 (Webb J).

112 Rocco Loiacono, 'New Human Rights Commissioner Warns on Vaccine Mandates', *The Spectator Australia*, November 25, 2021.

113 Ibid.

114 Rocco Loiacono, 'Most Covid Patients at Israeli Hospital Fully Vaccinated. What Does This Means for Australia?', *The Spectator Australia*, August 11, 2021.

115 Ibid.

116 Richard Furgason, 'Future Vaccine Should Be Mandatory, Says PM', *The Australian*, 19 August 2020.

117 Jade Gailberger, 'Coronavirus Vaccine Should Be Mandatory: PM', *PerthNow*, 19 August 2020.

118 Ibid.

119 Jack Phillips, 'Supermarkets Groceries Can Exclude Unvaccinated in Australian State: Official', *The Epoch Times*, December 10, 2021.

120 Michael Dimarco, 'Is political correctness responsible for our radical reactions to COVID-19?, *The Spectator*, September 2, 2021.

121 Conor Friedersdorf, "Australia Traded Away Too Much Liberty", *The Atlantic*, September 2, 2021.

122   Border Restrictions Direction (No. 43), September 18, 2021. This Direction is made under the Public Health Act 2005 (Qld).

123   Anton Nilsson & James O'Doherty, 'Covid 19 coronavirus Australia: NSW Health limits alcohol for residents of locked-down tower block', New Zealand Herald, September 9, 2021.

124   Elias Visontay, 'NSW unvaccinated could be denied freedoms at 80% target, premier says, as 1,257 Covid cases recorded", The Guardian, September 13, 2021.

125   R W Holder, *How Not To Say What You Mean: A Dictionary of Euphemisms* (4th ed, Oxford University Press, 2007) 269.

126   John Ayto and Ian Crofton, *Brewer's Dictionary of Modern Phrase and Fable* (2nd ed, London: Weidenfeld & Nicolson, 2006) 520.

127   Katherine Pratt, 'A Constructive Critique of Public Health Arguments for Antiobesity Soda Taxes and Food Taxes' (2012) 87 *Tulane Law Review* 73, 107.

128   'The new culture of dobbing', The Sydney Morning Herald, December 9, 2002.

129   Bruce Moore, 'The story of 'dob'', posted by Mark Gwynn on August 13, 2014, available at http://ozwords.org/?p=6426..

130   Donald Horne, *The Lucky Country* (Penguin Classics, 1964).

131   Donald Horne, *Death of the Lucky Country* (Penguin Classics, 1976).

132   (1992) 177 CLR 106, 108 ALR 577.

133   Ibid at [[212] (Gaudron J.)

134   John Locke, *Second Treatise on Civil Government* [1690], Chapter XI (Of the Extent of the Legislative Power), Sec. 134.

135   Ibid., Chapter IV (On Slavery), Sec. 23.

136   Samuel Rutherford, 'Lex Rex', or The Law and the Prince – Vol. 3, 34, in: *The Presbyterian Armoury*, 1846.

137   Charles E. Rice, *50 Questions on the Natural Law: What It Is and Why We Need It* (San Francisco/CA: Ignatius Press, 1999), 85.

138   Thomas Aquinas, *Summa Theologica,* 72, II, II, Q 104, art 6.

139   Ibid., 89, Bk 1, Ch 6.

140   Locke, above n.134, Section 222.

141   (1992) 177 CLR 1;108 ALR 681.

142   (1992) 177 CLR 1, at 48 (Brennan J.)

143   Ibid., at 49.

144   Caroline Schelle, 'COVID-19 Victoria: Anti-vaccine protesters rallied in Melbourne's CBD over coronavirus vaccine mandates', News.com.au, November 6, 2021.

145   Yoann Della Croce and Ophelia Nicole-Berva,' Civil Disobedience in Times of Pandemic: Clarifying Rights and Duties,' Criminal Law and Philosophy, July 28, 2021, 1-20.

146   Carl Cohen, 'Civil Disobedience and the Law' (1966) 21(1) *Rutgers Law Review* 4-5.

147   George Roberts, 'Almost half Australians can't read, write: Survey,' ABC News, February 2008.

148   Adam Carey, 'Rewarding,' but four in five teachers consider quitting in pandemic, The Age, October 29, 2021.

149   A.V. Dicey, Introduction to the Study of the Law of the Constitution [1885] (Liberty Fund, 1982) 107-122.

150   Hans Kelsen moved to the United States in 1940. In 1945, he was appointed full professor at the Department of Political Science at the University of California, Berkeley.

151   Hans Kelsen, Das Naturrecht in der Politischen Theorie (F M Schmoetz (ed) (1963). Quoted in Friederich A Hayek, *Law, Legislation and Liberty, Vol 2: The Mirage of Social Justice* (Routledge & Kegan Paul, 1976) 56.

152   Hans Kelsen, *Pure Theory of Law* (University of California Press, 1967) 40.

153   Mike Hawkins, *Social Darwinism in European and American Thought, 1860-1945* (Cambridge University Press, 1997) 90.

154   Karl Dietrich Bracher, *The German Dictatorship: The Origins, Structure and Effects of National Socialism* (Praeger Publishing, 1970) 474.

155   Frank Haldemann, 'Gustav Radbruch vs Hans Kelsen: A Debate on Nazi Law' (1958) 71 Harvard Law Review 162, 176.

156   Charles Rice, 'Some Reasons for a Restoration of Natural Law Jurisprudence' (1989) 24, *Wake Forest Law Review* 539, 567.

157   Heinrich Rommen, 'Natural Law Decisions of the Federal Supreme Court and of the Constitutional Courts in Germany' (1959), quoted in Charles Rice, *50 Questions on the Natural Law:*

What It Is and Why We Need It (Ignatius Press, 1999), 28.

158 Jeffrey Seitzer and Chris Thornhill, 'An Introduction to Carl Schmitt's Constitutional Theory: Issues and Context', in Jeffrey Seitzer (ed.), *Carl Schmitt: Constitutional Theory* (Duke University Press, 2008) 10.

159 Gustav Radbruch, 'Legal Philosophy' in K. Wilk (ed), *The Legal Philosophies of Lask, Radbruch, and Dabin (*Harvard University Press, 1950) 119.

160 J. M. Kelly, *A Short History of Western Legal Theory* (Oxford University Press, 1992) 379.

161 Gustav Radbruch, Rechtsphilosophie (K F Koehler Verlag, 1970). Quoted in Jes Bjarup , 'Continental Perspectives on Natural Law Theory and Legal Positivism', in M P Golding and W A Edmunson (eds), *The Blackwell Guide to the Philosophy of Law and Legal Theory* (Blackwell, 2005) 298.

162 Ibid.

163 Radbruch, Rechtsphilosophie (4th ed, 1950). Quoted in Kelly, above n 160, 419.

164 Ibid.

165 Ibid.

166 George Breckenridge, 'Legal Positivism and the Natural Law: The Controversy Between Professor Hart and Professor Fuller' (1964–1965) 18 *Vanderbilt Law Review* 945, 950.

167 R. C. van Caenegem, *An Historical Introduction to Western Constitutional Law* (Cambridge University Press, 1995), 283.

168 Ibid, 277.

169 Paul Johnson, *Modern Times: The World from the Twenties to the Nineties* (HarperPerennial, 2001) 111.

170 Ingo Müller, *Hitler's Justice: The Courts of the Third Reich* (Harvard University Press, 1991) 38.

171 Gerhard Fieberg, *Justiz im Nationalsozialistischen Deutschland* (1984), 37 quoted in Müller, above n 182, 38.

172 Friedrich Roetter, 'The Impact of Nazi Law' (1945) *Wisconsin Law Review* 516, 542.

173 Caenegem, above n 167, 284.

174 Hans Frank, Reichsgesetzblatt (1933), 39. Quoted in Michael

Stolleis, *The Law Under the Swastika: Studies on Legal History in Nazi Germany* (University of Chicago Press, 1998) 14.

175   Martin Broszat, *The Hitler State: The Foundation and Development of the Internal Structure of the Third Reich* (Longman, 1981), 293.

176   Johnson, above n 169, 290.

177   K. C. H. Willig, 'The Bar in the Third Reich' (1976) 20 *American Journal of Legal History* 13, 14.

178   Müller, above n 170, 38.

179   Ibid.

180   Matthew Lippman, 'Law, Lawyers and Legality in the Third Reich: The Perversion of Principle and Professionalism' (1997) 11(2) *Temple International and Comparative Law Journal* 199, 206.

181   Edwin W. Lutzer, *Hitler's Cross: How the Cross was Used to Promote the Nazi Agenda* (Moody Publishers, 2012), 46.

182   Laurence Rees, *The Dark Charisma of Adolf Hitler: Leading Millions into the Abyss* (Ebury Press, 2013), 66.

183   Ibid.

184   Ibid, 269.

185   Ibid, 233.

186   Michael E Tigar and John Mage, 'The Reichstag Fire Trial, 1933–2008: The Production of Law and History' (2009) 60, *Monthly Review* 24, 46.

187   Müller, above n 170, 196.

188   Ibid, 41.

189   Maxilimiam Rottleuthner, 'Legal Positivism and National Socialism: A Contribution to a Theory of Legal Development' (2011) 12 *German Law Journal* 100, 108.

190   Erich Schultze, 'Zeitspiegel' (1933) 25 Deutsche Richterzeitung 258, cited in Müller, above n 170, 38.

191   Ibid, 37.

192   'Richter und Staatanwalt im Dritten Reich' (1933) 280, quoted in Müller, above n 170, 38.

193   Müller, above note 170, 116.

194   Ibid, 134.

195   Markus Dirk Dubber, 'Judicial Positivism and Hitler's Injustice' (1993) 93 (7) *Columbia Law Review* 1807, 1824.

196   Judith N Shklar, *Legalism: Law, Morals, and Political Trials* (2nd ed, Harvard University Press, 1986), 72.

197   M Koessler, 'Nazi Justice and the Democratic Approach: The Debasement of Germany's Legal System' (1950) 36 *ABA Journal* 634, p 635.

198   Hans Kelsen, *General Theory of Law and State* (Harvard University Press, 1946) 391.

199   Ibid, 1.

200   Friedrich Carl von Savigny, *On the Vocation of Our Age For Legislation and Jurisprudence* (trans A Hayward, London, 1831) 152.

201   Abraham Kuyper, *Lectures on Calvinism* (Hendrickson, 2008) 75.

202   Richard Overy, *Dictators: Hitler's Germany and Stalin's Russia* (Allen Lane, 2004) 289.

203   Ibid, 290.

204   Karl Loewenstein, 'Law in the Third Reich' (1936) 45 *Yale Law Journal* 779, 784.

205   Leo Strauss, *Natural Right and History* (Chicago University Press, 1965), 3.

206   Ibid, 18.

207   Andreas Rahmatian, 'Friedrich Carl von Savigny's Beruf und Volksgeistlehre' (2007) *Journal of Legal History* 1, 12.

208   Loewenstein, above n 204, 784.

209   Stolleis, above n 174, 98–9.

210   Ernst Forsthoff, Der totale Staat, 26 cited in Müller, above n 182, 71.

211   Loewenstein, above n 204, 803.

212   Johnson, above n 169, 117.

213   Hence, two years later the Reichstag introduced on 15 September 1935 its notorious 'Law for the Procreation of German Blood and German Honour', which prohibited the marriage between Jews and citizens of Germany or 'related kinds of blood'. Marriages contracted in violation of that law were null and void. Two other laws were passed by the Reichstag, one depriving individuals

'not of German blood' of their rights as citizens, and another prohibiting, among other things, marriages between Jews and citizens of German or related kinds of blood': see Law for the Protection of German Blood and German Honour, 15 September 1935, at 8 September 2009; see also The Reich Citizenship Law, 15 September 1935, at <http://frank.mtsu.edu/~baustin/nurmlaw2.html>.

214   Loewenstein, above n 204, 786.

215   Ibid.

216   Karl Binding and Alfred Hoche, Die Freigabe der Vernichtung Lebensunwerten Lebens, 1920, 40 cited in Müller, above n 170, 121.

217   Stolleis, above n 174, 91.

218   Aurel Kolnai, The War Against the West (Viking Press, 1938), 300.

219   Ian Kershaw, *Hitler: A Profile in Power* (Longman, 1991), 78.

220   Müller, above n 170, 42.

221   Seitzer and Thornhill, above n 158, 13.

222   Ibid, 14.

223   Laurence Rees, *The Dark Charisma of Adolf Hitler: Leading Millions into the Abyss* (Ebury Press, 2013), 144.

224   Carl Schmitt, 'Der Begriff des Politischen' (1927) 58 Archiv für Sozialwissenschaft und Sozialpolitik 1-33, quoted in Richard Pipes, *Russia Under the Bolshevik Regime* (Vintage Books, 1995), 263.

225   These special powers remained in effect for four years, after which they could be renewed if the state of emergency was still in place. Whether or not the fire was really set by the communists, the fact is that that section served the purposes of the declaration of a state of emergency.

226   Its preamble declared: 'As provided for by Article 48, paragraph 2 of the Constitution, the following is decreed to defend the state against Communist acts of violence ...'

227   Richard J Evans, *The Third Reich in Power: 1933–1939* (Penguin Books, 2006) 6.

228   Such a 'further notice' did not occur until May 8, 1945, when the decree was finally cancelled by the military government of the

Allies.

229 Carl Schmitt, *Politische Theologie* (2nd ed, 1934) 20 cited in Müller, above n 170, 46.

230 Hitler saw the independence of the SA and its penchant for street violence as a threat to his newly gained political power. Most of the killings were carried out by the SS and the Gestapo, the regime's secret police.

231 William L. Shirer, *The Rise and Fall of the Third Reich* (Rosetta Books, 2001), 111.

232 In a 13 July speech, Hitler declared: 'In this hour, I was responsible for the fate of the German nation and thereby the Supreme Law Lord (Hoechster Gerichtsherr) of the German people' - Loewenstein, above n 204, 811.

233 Carl Schmitt, 'Der Führer Schützt das Recht' (1934) Deutsche Juristen-Zeitung 947. Quoted in Loewenstein, above n 204, 811.

234 'Carl Schmitt … developed a theoretical account of international law that brought raw power to centre stage, a kind of right-wing Marxism in which instead of economic activity forming the determining base for all aspects of human society and human history, that foundational role was reserved for executive decision making. Schmitt's was an extreme version of the capitulation of international law to power, yet it illustrates the conundrum: international law is at the same time about power, and not about power' - John R Morss, 'Power and International Law: Hohfeld to the Rescue?' (2011) 2 *The Western Australian Jurist* 93, 100.

235 (1949) 79 CLR 201, at 293 (Webb J).

236 Ibid.

237 Friedrich A. Hayek, *Law, Legislation and Liberty*, Vol. 3 (University of Chicago Press, 1981), Ch. 17.

238 'Research Starters: Worldwide Deaths in World War II', The National WWII Museum of New Orleans.

239 COVID-19 Omnibus (Emergency Measures) and Other Acts Amendment Bill 2020, Victorian Legislation.

240 Ian Hanke, 'Daniel Andrews' Plan For Indefinite Detention – And More', *The Spectator Australia,* 18 September 2020.

241 'Benjamin Franklin on trade off between essential liberty and temporary safety (1775)', Liberty Fund.

ABOUT THE AUTHORS

Professor Augusto Zimmermann is Professor of Law and Head of Law at the Sheridan Institute of Higher Education, Perth. He is also Adjunct Professor of Law at the University of Notre Dame Australia, Sydney campus. In addition, Professor Zimmermann is a former Law Reform Commissioner with the Law Reform Commission of Western Australian (2012-2017) and a former Associate Dean (Research) and Postgraduate Research Director at Murdoch University's School of Law. Professor Zimmermann is also the founder and President of the Western Australian Legal Theory Association (WALTA), a former Vice-President of the Australasian Society of Legal Philosophy (ASLP), an Elected Fellow at the International Academy for the Study of the Jurisprudence of the Family, and Editor-in-Chief of the Western Australian Jurist law journal. A prolific writer and the author of numerous articles and academic books, he was awarded the 2012 Vice Chancellor's Award for Excellence in Research, and two School Dean's Research Awards, in 2010 and 2011. Professor Zimmermann served on numerous academic bodies at Murdoch, including: the Research Degree and Scholarships Committee; the Vice Chancellor's Awards and Citations Committee; the Academic Council's Freedom of Speech in Policies and Procedures Advisory Group; and the Academic Staff Promotions Advisory Committee. In January 2015, he was invited by the Tasmanian Chief Justice to address the 'Opening of the Legal Year' in that State. Professor Zimmermann is generally recognised as a fierce advocate for free speech and the Rule of Law, contributing with numerous articles on the subject, including for *The Legal Doctrines of the Rule of Law and the Legal State (Rechtsstaat)* (Springer, 2014), a book edited by the President of the American Bar Association (ABA) that explores the development of both the civil law and the common law conceptions of the Rule of Law. He is the author/co-author/editor/co-editor of numerous academic articles and books, including *Fundamental Rights in the Age of Covid-19* (Connor Court Publishing, 2021); *No Offence Intended: Why 18C is Wrong* (Connor Court Publishing, 2016); *Christian Foundations of the Common Law* (3 Volumes, Connor Court Publishing, 2018); *Global Perspectives on Subsidiarity* (Springer, 2014); and *Western Legal Theory: History, Concepts and Perspectives* (LexisNexis, 2013). Finally, Professor Zimmermann has been included, together with only twelve other Australian academics and policy experts, in 'Policy Experts' – the Heritage Foundation's directory for locating knowledgeable authorities and leading policy institutes actively involved in a broad range of public policy issues, both in the United States and worldwide.

Professor Gabriël A. Moens AM is Emeritus Professor of Law, The University of Queensland. He served as Pro Vice Chancellor, Dean and Professor of Law, Murdoch University. He also served as Head, Graduate School of Law, The University of Notre Dame Australia; Garrick Professor of Law, The University of Queensland; and Professor of Law, Curtin University. In 1999, Professor Moens received the Australian Award for University Teaching in Law and Legal Studies. In 2003, the Prime Minister of Australia awarded him the Australian Centenary Medal for services to education. He was named the "International Alumnus of the Year" by the Pritzker Law School of Northwestern University, Chicago in 2019. In June 2019 he was appointed a Member of the Order of Australia (AM) for services to the law and higher education. Professor Moens is a Membre Titulaire, International Academy of Comparative Law, Paris; a Fellow of the Australian Institute of Management (WA); a Fellow of the College of Law; a Fellow of the Australian Academy of Law; and a Fellow of the Australian Centre for International Commercial Arbitration. He is author/co-author/editor/co-editor of *Enduring Ideas*, Connor Court Publishing 2020; *Law of International Business in Australasia* (2nd ed), The Federation Press, 2019; *The Constitution of the Commonwealth of Australia Annotated* (9th ed), LexisNexis Butterworths, 2016; *Arbitration and Dispute Resolution in the Resources Sector: An Australian Perspective*, Springer, 2015; *Jurisprudence of Liberty* (2nd ed), LexisNexis, 2011; *Commercial Law of the European Union*, Springer, 2010; and *International Trade and Business: Law, Policy and Ethics* (2nd ed), Routledge/Cavendish, 2006. His debut novel *A Twisted Choice*, a thriller exploring the origins of COVID-19, was published in 2020 by Boolarong Press, which also published a short story, *The Greedy Prospector*, in an anthology of short stories in 2021. His second novel, *The Coincidence*, was published by Connor Court Publishing in

2021. He writes opinion pieces and commentary for various magazines and newspapers.

www.ingramcontent.com/pod-product-compliance
Lightning Source LLC
Chambersburg PA
CBHW021715210326
41599CB00013B/1655